The LANGUAGE *of* PUBLISHING

AN·TO·Z GLOSSARY
OF BOOK PUBLISHING TERMS

Manhattan Beach, California

The content in this book is adapted from "The Language of Publishing," a series of articles written by Linda Carlson that was originally published in IBPA's *Independent* magazine. The original articles, along with hundreds of other useful articles, are available in the *Independent* archives at www.ibpa-online.org.

Every effort has been made to ensure that all the information in this book is accurate at the time of publication; however, IBPA neither endorses nor guarantees the content of external links referenced in this book.

If you have questions or comments about this book, or need information about licensing, custom editions, special sales, or academic/corporate purchases, please contact the Independent Book Publishers Association.

Published by the Independent Book Publishers Association (IBPA)
1020 Manhattan Beach Blvd., Suite 204
Manhattan Beach, CA 90266
www.IBPA-online.org
310-546-1818
info@IBPA-online.org

Written by Linda Carlson
Cover Design by Dunn+Associates; Interior Design by TLC Graphics
Editing by Audrey Lintner; Proofreading by Lawrence W. Baker and Peter Vogt
Printing by Ingram Lightning Source

Stock art: pg. 11, Vectorious; pg. 48, Dover

First Edition
ISBN (print): 978-1-938646-01-0
ISBN (e-book): 978-1-938646-02-7

Printed in the United States of America

INTRODUCTION

For the past 30 years, the Independent Book Publishers Association (IBPA) has been helping indie presses and self-published authors understand the ins and outs of publishing so they can compete in a meaningful way. With the publication of *The Language of Publishing: An A-to-Z Glossary of Book Publishing Terms*, we're pleased to add another powerful tool to the indie publisher's toolkit.

There is nothing more fundamental to success in an industry than a practical understanding of its terms and jargon. The words defined here are the ones you need to know because they are the ones you use. If you are a newcomer to publishing, you may be mystified by its vocabulary and fearful of what might happen if you confuse gutters with margins or signatures with units. If you are established in your business, you may still be struggling to understand pixels vs. picas, line screens vs. dpi, or RGB vs. CMYK. And all of us sometimes have to deal with an author, an employee, or a customer who needs a translation of traditional publishing terms.

This is why IBPA developed *The Language of Publishing*. This book provides the foundation one needs to speak intelligently with designers, book manufacturers, wholesalers, POD specialists, and many others.

With all the changes taking place in publishing today, it is nice to know there is a resource to turn to for authoritative information and advice. IBPA is proud to serve as this resource for our 3,000 members. We welcome you to our community.

Angela Bole
Executive Director
Independent Book Publishers Association
Manhattan Beach, CA

AUTHOR ACKNOWLEDGMENTS

When *The Language of Publishing* ran as a series of articles in IBPA's *Independent* magazine, the magazine's staff received a great deal of positive feedback from both those new to publishing and industry veterans.

We created this helpful resource with the assistance of many. IBPA members suggested terms that had confused them or their new employees, and several members shared the resources they had compiled. I am particularly grateful to Joel Friedlander for the terms defined in his post "The Language of the Book" at www.thebookdesigner.com, and I extend many thanks to Pete Masterson, who provided both encouragement and a copy of his detailed *Book Design and Production*. Industry specialists, especially book manufacturers, suggested terms often misunderstood by customers, and helped me write definitions that make sense to all of us, whether we predate ISBNs or are new to publishing. Many of these were colleagues of Judith Appelbaum, the *Independent*'s longstanding editor who is always a source of valuable contacts.

It was with the assistance and enthusiasm of so many people that it was possible to create this resource that answers dozens of questions about design, production, distribution, royalties, discounts, and other factors that can make the difference between struggling and succeeding in publishing. Many thanks to you all.

Linda Carlson
Staff Reporter
IBPA's *Independent* magazine
Seattle, WA

●　●　●　●　●　●　●　●　●　●　●　●　●　●　●　●　●　●　●　●

NOTE TO READERS

We have worked hard to ensure this glossary is user-friendly. To this end, we have included multiple cross references for your benefit. All cross references have been noted in **_BOLD, ITALICIZED CAPS_**. If you have the eBook edition, all cross references are also hyperlinked.

●　●　●　●　●　●　●　●　●　●　●　●　●　●　●　●　●　●　●　●

ACID FREE: Paper made in a neutral pH system to increase its longevity. A pH level from 0 to 7 is classified as acid, 7 to 14 as alkaline. Acid-free or neutral paper includes at least 2 percent calcium carbonate.

ACQUISITIONS or COLLECTION DEVELOPMENT: The library department to be contacted regarding purchase of a title.

ACQUISITIONS EDITOR: In larger publishing operations, the staff member who finds viable book projects, recommends (and sometimes decides) which books to buy, and handles contract negotiations. In companies that publish such nonfiction as how-to and computer guides, the acquisitions editor may be responsible for finding authors for particular topics the company has determined are marketable.

ACROBAT: The Adobe software used to create files in *PORTABLE DOCUMENT FORMAT (PDF)*. PDFs are opened with Adobe Reader, a different program. PDFs can be created with various levels of quality, the highest appropriate for printing and the lowest appropriate for websites and email. Book manufacturers may specify what level must be used.

ADD-ON BAR CODE: Provides information not included in the main *EAN/UPC* bar code symbol such as a book's

$29.95

ISBN 978-0-9863738-0-0

9 780986 373800   5 2 9 9 5

SAMPLE

An ADD-ON BAR CODE, showing the five-digit price on the right.

price. The add-on symbol is displayed to the right of the main bar code. Add-on codes for books are usually five digits and start with the number 5.

ADVANCE: A payment a publisher makes to an author prior to publication of a book and usually prior to delivery of the manuscript. The advance is against earned royalties, which means the author will not receive an additional payment until the advance is *EARNED OUT.* If the advance is $500, for example, and the royalty per book is $1, the publisher must have net sales of 500 books before the author gets the first royalty payment.

ADVANCE SHIP NOTICE: See *ASN*.

AFTERWORD: A comment in the *END MATTER*, usually written by someone other than the author. Similar to an *EPILOGUE*.

AGAINST THE GRAIN: At a right angle to the direction of the fiber in a sheet of paper. Folding with (rather than against) the grain is recommended because it creates a better, flatter crease. When pages are printed so that a book is bound against the grain, they curl at least slightly.

ALTERATION: A change made in the text or images on *GAL-LEYS* or *PAGE PROOFS*. The cost of making "author alterations" (AAs) may be charged to the author.

APPENDIX: Reference or additional material in the *END MATTER*.

APPLICATION FILES: Software—such as QuarkXpress, Adobe In-Design, Photoshop, Illustrator, and *FONT* files—used to create a book. Book manufacturers (aka printers) may ask that application files be submitted along with ***PDFs.***

APRON: Extra blank space at the binding edge of a foldout, usually on a ***FRENCH FOLD,*** which allows an oversize page separate from a ***SIGNATURE*** to be folded and ***TIPPED IN*** (that is, glued in between the pages of a signature, or between signatures) so that all the text or illustrations on the foldout can be seen. Maps and family trees are examples of images often created as foldouts, with an extra-wide margin on the binding edge.

ARC: Advance reader (or readers or reading) copy, a prepublication version of a book for use by booksellers and reviewers. ARCs may lack images and final ***COPYEDITING.*** Today they're often available in digital form or via ***PRINT-ON-DEMAND (POD).***

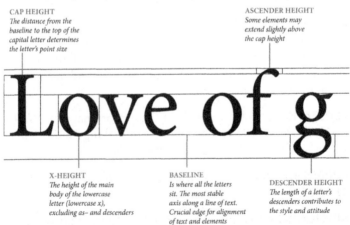

CAP HEIGHT
The distance from the baseline to the top of the capital letter determines the letter's point size

ASCENDER HEIGHT
Some elements may extend slightly above the cap height

X-HEIGHT
The height of the main body of the lowercase letter (lowercase x), excluding as– and descenders

BASELINE
Is where all the letters sit. The most stable axis along a line of text. Crucial edge for alignment of text and elements

DESCENDER HEIGHT
The length of a letter's descenders contributes to the style and attitude

The ASCENDER rises above the height of lower-case letters, or x-height.

ASCENDER: Ascenders are the parts of letters that rise above the height of lower-case letters, like the upward-extending parts of the *l, f,* or *t*. Contrast with descenders, the parts that extend below the ***BASELINE,*** as in the "tail" of the letter *y, g,* or *p*. When type is ***LEADED*** tightly (for example, 9-point type on 9 ***POINTS*** of space), the descenders of one line may overlap the ascenders of the next.

ASN: Advance ship notice, usually sent electronically in a standard format. It announces a pending delivery.

B2B: Business-to-business sales; by a publisher, for example, to a retailer or library, sometimes through a *WHOLESALER* or *DISTRIBUTOR*.

B2C: Business-to-consumer sales by a business directly to an end user.

BACKBONE: Book *SPINE*.

BACKLIST: Older titles. Publishers that issue new titles twice annually may consider spring titles to be backlist when fall titles are issued. Other publishers consider titles *FRONTLIST* for a year or longer, and some independent publishers prefer to keep all their titles *EVERGREEN*.

BACK MATTER: The parts of a book that appear after the main text; for instance, bibliography, index, and appendices. Also called *END MATTER*.

BACKORDER: An order placed when a book is not available, to be fulfilled when it is in stock. Backorders often come in when a new title or a new reprint is on the way.

BACKSTORY: What happened before a book's story starts. Similar to a *PREQUEL*. The term is also used to describe an author's account of writing a particular book.

BAD BREAK: A word broken incorrectly at the end of a line. Also refers to a line of text or a *SUBHEAD* that is placed on the page in a way that is unattractive or misleading. Types of bad breaks include the **WIDOW**, when a short last line of a paragraph appears at the top of a column or page; the **ORPHAN**, when a short first line of a paragraph appears at the end of a column or page; a subhead that appears at the bottom of a column or page; and a hyphen break at the end of the last line on a page. Starting a new line between or after initials in a name also creates a bad break.

BANNER: In print, one name for the title of a periodical as displayed on the front cover of a magazine or the first page of a newspaper or newsletter. The banner includes the publication's name, volume, date, number, and serial information. To qualify a periodical for mailing at special rates, the periodical's masthead must display this information within the first five pages, or on the table of contents or editorial pages. In online advertising, banners are large display ads (rather than text, or classified ads), often spanning the width of the screen. Vertical banners are usually called skyscrapers.

BAR CODE: Most retailers and all **WHOLESALERS** require that back covers of books carry a bar code for the **ISBN** in a prescribed size and color, usually black on white. Today many books also carry a **QR CODE**, the square code that smartphones and tablets can read and that usually leads to a source of additional information.

BASELINE: The imaginary line on which type sits, although descenders extend below the baseline.

BEA: BookExpo America, the major U.S. publishing event, originally the annual convention of the American Booksellers Association. Held each year in late May/early June.

BIBLIOGRAPHY: The by-author list of publications cited in, or relating to the topic of, a book. Part of the *END MATTER*.

BINDING: *FOLDING*, trimming, and attaching pages of a book with adhesives, sewing, stitching, plastic or metal coils, metal prongs, or snaps. The bindery is also where perforating, embossing, *DIE-CUTTING*, and other such specialty work is done. With digital printing, two different binding methods are possible. Inline binding, available only for paperbacks, involves a print engine that feeds the *BOOK BLOCK* directly to a binding unit, a three-knife trimmer, and then a packing and boxing station. Offline binding equipment, which is separate from the press, usually involves a process similar to the manufacture of *OFFSET* publications: books are printed before they go to the bindery, and binding can be *PERFECT*, *SADDLE-STITCHED*, *MECHANICAL*, or *CASEBOUND*. Today many book manufacturers contract out case binding, which means your hardcover book will physically be moved from one plant to another. In most cases, *LIBRARY BINDING* is done not by book manufacturers, but by specialty binderies. If you offer titles with library binding, you must order extra covers for this process. The term *binding* also means the edge of a book that is bound (binding edge).

BISAC CODES: The familiar term for the BISAC (Book Industry Standards and Communications) Subject Headings used to categorize books according to their subjects and to standardize the electronic transfer of subject information between publishers and booksellers. The complete BISAC Subject Headings list is free for book-by-book lookup at *bisg.org*.

BLAD: Book *LAYOUT* and design. A printed sample used by sales reps to sell a title in advance of publication. It often features sections from the finished book, including cover artwork, page layouts, and images. Most commonly used today for children's picture books.

BLEED: An image or text that extends ("bleeds") over one or more edges of a page. Publishers asking printers for quotes on a book with cover or text bleeds must specify how many bleeds it will have; for example, "cover bleeds one side" or "cover bleeds four sides." A full-bleed image extends (that is, bleeds) over all the edges so there is no unprinted *GUTTER* or margin. Most printers

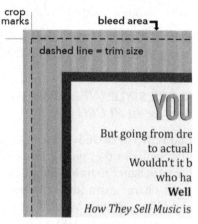

The BLEED area extends beyond the trim.

require that artwork extend at least an eighth of an inch (a quarter inch for digital printed or *WEB PRESS* jobs) past the *TRIM* line to ensure the margin is completely covered with ink. Bleeds across gutters (i.e., between the two pages of a spread) are not available with digital printing. Because paper is wasted with bleeds, printers charge more for jobs with them. The term also describes ink that has spread into parts of the page where it should not.

BLEEDTHROUGH: When one side of a sheet is heavily inked, the paper may absorb so much ink that the type or images can be seen on the reverse side. More common with thin paper, bleedthrough should be corrected at the ***PRESS CHECK.***

BLIND EMBOSSING: A printing technique in which a bas-relief design is created without ***FOIL*** or ink.

BLIND FOLIO: A page number that is assigned to a page (such as the title page and other ***FRONT MATTER*** pages) but not printed on it.

BLOCK STYLE: When all lines of a piece of text, including the first, are set ***FLUSH*** left.

BLUELINE or BLUES: The final one-color, print-on-paper copy of a book or other publication before it goes to the press, and the last chance to fix anything that needs fixing. Printers sometimes charge extra for a blueline, which is made from ***FILM*** and light-sensitive paper. Any changes made at the blueline stage are expensive. Also called a silverprint, brownline, or Van Dyke. With digital reproduction, there is no film; instead, you can check the ***LASER PRINT.***

BLURB: An endorsement, often by someone well known, used in the ***FRONT MATTER,*** the cover, and promotional material.

BOARD BOOK: Made with sturdy, cardboard-type pages and covers. Usually for young children, and limited in number of pages.

BOLDFACE: Thicker, visually heavier or darker type. In desktop publishing programs such as InDesign, the *STROKE MENU* can be used to further increase the thickness of type.

BOOK BLOCK: The pages of a book after they have been printed and *FOLDED AND GATHERED* but before the cover is attached. With *SHEET-FED* digital presses, the book block is a stack of single pages. With *OFFSET* presses, either *SHEET-FED* or *WEB*, the block is a stack of partial or full *SIGNATURES*.

BOOK DESIGNER: A graphic designer with specialized experience in book design and an understanding of book manufacturing.

BOOK DOCTOR: A consultant who edits a manuscript in terms of basic structure and content. A book doctor may be hired by an author to get a manuscript ready for submission to a publisher, or by a publisher with a manuscript that needs significant work.

BOOKEXPO AMERICA: See *BEA*.

BOOK PACKAGER: Traditionally an individual or a company that assembled the components of a book (including text, images, design, and possibly related materials, such as implements or materials used in the projects described in the book) and marketed the package to a publisher. Today often used to refer to businesses that assemble the components of a book (possibly on a *WORK-FOR-HIRE* basis) as well as related merchandise (such as a children's toy) and produce the package for private labeling by an organization (a museum's gift store, for example).

BOOK PAPER: A general term for papers most suitable for book manufacture.

BOOKS IN PRINT: The R.R. Bowker database to which publishers submit ISBNs for books in print and in production. See *bowker link.com*.

BOUND GALLEYS: Originally, pages of a book in almost final form that were bound together and distributed for reviews. Now usually replaced by bound *PAGE PROOFS*. See also *ARC*.

BRIGHTNESS: A technical measurement of the light reflected by paper, expressed in the United States by the 0 to 100 scale of the Technical Association of the Pulp and Paper Industry. A higher number means brighter paper.

BROADSIDE: An illustration or a table that is so wide it must be turned 90 degrees counterclockwise to fit on a page. The same as landscape orientation.

BULKING: The measurement of paper thickness expressed in terms of how many pages equal one inch, as in "360 ppi" (360 pages per inch). A lower PPI (high-bulk sheets) will create a thicker book; a higher PPI (low-bulk sheets) will create a thinner one. Book manufacturers use the PPI and the *COVER STOCK* thickness to determine *SPINE* width, which determines what size type and image can be used on a book's spine. Determining the bulk of a book is also done with a bulking dummy, made up of unprinted sheets of the specified paper folded in the *SIGNATURE* size and signature number of the job.

CALIPER: The thickness of a sheet of paper, in thousandths of an inch (*POINTS* or mils).

CALLOUT: A reference in text to a numbered figure or table (e.g., "see Figure 1"). During *COPYEDITING*, callouts are inserted properly in text, and figures and tables are placed as close as possible to their callouts.

CAMERA-READY ART or CRA: Material (text with or without illustrations and photographs) ready to be imaged onto *FILM*. Until electronic preproduction, CRA for *OFFSET* reproduction was prepared as *PASTEUPS* or *PHOTOSTATS*. Today most camera-ready art is submitted electronically, often as *PDF*s.

CANDLESTICK: *SADDLE-STITCHED* or stapled binding. Often used for children's paperbacks and magazines.

CAPTION: Text accompanying a photo or illustration.

CARET: The *COPYEDITING* or *PROOFREADING* mark that indicates the insertion point for additional text.

CASEBOUND: *HARDCOVER*, hardbound.

CENTER SPREAD: The facing pages in the center of a bound *SIGNATURE*.

CHANNELS: In publishing, channels refers to sales channels, which are usually trade (through *DISTRIBUTORS* and *WHOLESALERS* to bookstores and libraries, or direct to bookstores and libraries), and specialty (nonbook distributors and retailers such as gift reps and toy and health food stores). Another channel is direct to consumer through **DIRECT MAIL**, websites, and author appearances or speeches.

CHAPTER BOOK: A book for children who can read, usually longer than the 32 pages typical of picture books.

CHARACTER: A single letter, number, symbol, or blank space.

CHARACTER COUNT: The number of characters in a defined area such as a line of text or a page.

CHECK COPY: A **FOLDED AND GATHERED (F&G)** but unbound copy of a book sent by the book manufacturer to the publisher for approval prior to binding. F&Gs can be used in the bindery as guides for assembling books with any extra items such as **COLOR INSERTS** or CDs.

CHECK DIGIT: The final digit in an ISBN to validate that all its digits are correct.

CHOKES AND SPREADS: Called **TRAPPING** in desktop publishing and other digital imaging systems, these create overlaps to avoid a gap around image detail when different ink colors are used. If title type is set in yellow, for example, trapping ensures that the background color slightly overlaps the yellow so that all the paper is covered even if **COLOR SEPA-RATIONS** are slightly misaligned on the press. When a darker color surrounds a lighter color, the term is spread (e.g., a red cover surrounding the yellow type of the title); the term is choke when a lighter color—say, a yellow cover—surrounds what's in the middle (e.g., a red image).

CHROMALIN PROOFS: Proof copy, often of a cover, made with photosensitized clear plastic and processed in layers of color to simulate the final printed image.

CIBACHROME: A full-color positive photographic print made from a *TRANSPARENCY.*

CIP: Library of Congress Cataloging in Publication data: a bibliographic record prepared by the Library of Congress for a book before its publication. The CIP data should be included on the book's *COPYRIGHT* page. See "Cataloging in Publication Program," *loc.gov/publish/cip.*

C/LC, C&LC, CLC: *COPYEDITING* or *PROOFREADING* abbreviations: the instruction to set the first letter of each word (excluding articles, conjunctions, and prepositions) as a cap (i.e., capital or upper-case letter) and the other letters in lower case.

CLIP ART: Stock illustrations (once sold on large sheets from which the desired image could be cut, or clipped; now sold online as digital files or individually on stock photography sites) that can be used instead of commissioned artwork. Some clip art is free; some must be purchased. Not all clip art is available in the *HIGH-RESOLUTION* graphics files needed for good-quality reproduction, especially if it is scanned from vintage advertisements or books.

High-resolution
CLIP ART

CMYK: Four inks—cyan (blue), magenta (red), yellow, and black (key)—are used to build colors with ***FOUR-COLOR PRINTING***. In digital printing, ***PANTONE MATCHING SYSTEM® (PMS®)*** ink colors are usually converted to CMYK. This can cause color variations between digitally printed jobs and ***OFFSET*** jobs, where PMS® colors can be matched. Because computer monitors display colors in RGB format (red/green/blue), it is impossible to accurately proof CMYK or PMS® colors with a digital display or with prints made with a laser or inkjet printer. For CMYK, a designer should provide the book manufacturer with a printed example of the color to be matched. If PMS® colors are specified, paper swatches should be provided with the ***COMPS***.

COATING: Many new digital presses include coating as one step of the printing process. This protects the ink and reduces scuffing and fingerprinting. Because digital toners are not always compatible with coatings, many digitally printed book covers are ***LAMINATED*** rather than ***UV-COATED*** or ***VARNISHED***. ***SPOT COATINGS*** target one part of a page, such as one color, one image, or the text. Flood coatings cover the entire page. Coatings can be gloss or ***MATTE*** (dull).

COIL BOUND: A binding that requires punching (drilling) holes in a book and inserting a metal or plastic coil to keep pages together. Coil bound is a process not available inline (that is, as part of the printing process on a sophisticated press or print-on-demand equipment such as the ***ESPRESSO BOOK MACHINE***). Booksellers are often reluctant to carry coil-bound books unless they are ***SHRINK-WRAPPED*** or otherwise packaged to reduce the chance of damage. Coil-bound books have another disadvantage: no **SPINE** to show title and author.

COLLATE: Gather sections in sequence for binding.

COLOR BARS: Printed bars of ink colors used to monitor a print image. These bars show the amount of ink to be applied by the press, the **REGISTRATION**, and the **DENSITIES** across the press sheet.

COLOR FASTNESS: The ability of dyed paper to maintain color when exposed to light or heat.

COLOR INSERT: To reduce the cost of printing high-quality photos in color, all the color photographs for a book can be printed in one or more **SIGNATURES** separately from the text (which is usually printed with black ink) and then inserted in the book, often in the center, at the bindery. Because of the high cost of high-quality color printing, some publishers order **OVERRUNS** of color inserts with the original printing for use when a book is reprinted.

COLOR KEY: An **OVERLAY PROOF** with just one color per sheet of acetate.

COLOR PROOFS: The first few sheets pulled off the press for the customer's final approval before the entire job is printed. This **PRESS CHECK** is often done by the book designer or **PRODUCTION MANAGER**.

COLOR SEPARATION: In a multicolor print job, each component color requires its own monochrome image. A film negative is made from each of these monochrome images for **OFFSET** and **LETTERPRESS** printing. A two-color job requires two **SEPARATIONS**; a **FOUR-COLOR** job requires four if **PROCESS COLOR** (see **CMYK**) is being used. A multicolor job using several **PANTONE MATCHING SYSTEM®** **(PMS®)** inks but no full-color images would have a separation for each PMS® color.

COLUMN: Text arranged in a vertical segment, usually narrower than the width of the page. The space between columns is called a **DITCH**.

COMB BOUND: A binding that uses a plastic, spring-like comb inserted through holes punched in the edges of book pages. It is not popular with bookstores because of the risk of damage to the plastic. See also **COIL BOUND**.

COMPS: Comprehensive **LAYOUTS** are the second visual step in the creative process, after **THUMBNAILS** (rough miniature sketches). The comp of a book cover, interior design, ad, or other promotional piece is an early draft that shows color, **FONTS**, and at least rough images. **LOW-RESOLUTION STOCK PHOTOS** and **GREEKED TEXT** are common. A comprehensive proof shows material as it will look when printed. Today comps are often presented electronically, as either **JPEG** or **PDF** files.

CONDENSED TYPE: **TYPEFACES** with tall, narrow characters that allow more characters per line (in contrast to **EXPANDED FACE**, which permits fewer characters per line). Desktop publishing programs such as InDesign allow designers to further reduce space between letters and between words.

CONSIGNMENT SALES: When **DISTRIBUTORS, WHOLE-SALERS**, and retailers do not pay publishers until books are sold to readers. Technically, the publisher retains legal ownership until a sale is final. In reality, however, if a distributor, wholesaler, or retailer goes bankrupt, the books in its possession are usually considered its assets and are liquidated to pay secured creditors. The exception occurs when a publisher has filed a Uniform Commercial Code financing statement for each title and each consignment customer. For details, see your state's UCC regulations.

CONTINUOUS TONE/CONTONE: Images with a range of tones from white to black that may have every shade of gray represented, as in traditional photography. In *OFFSET* printing, continuous-tone images are converted *(SCREENED)* to *HALFTONES* for reproduction. Many digital color laser presses are contone printers. Limited in the levels of intensity they can produce, they use *DITHERING* techniques to create different colors and different shades of lightness and darkness. For example, dots of different red, cream, and white shades might be used to create a pattern

A CONTINUOUS TONE image showing a wide range of grays.

that makes the eye think it is seeing pink. Similar to halftones.

CO-PUBLISHING: A venture in which two or more organizations, or an organization and an individual, share the development and/or production costs of publishing a book. For example, a museum underwrites some of the costs of a book about its collection published by a university press. Today the term is often used by publishers or **BOOK PACKAGERS** who expect authors to bear some of the costs of producing a book.

COPYEDITING: Copyeditors are responsible for **STYLE** (for example, which abbreviations are used, how numbers are referred to, and which words are hyphenated), for consistency throughout a manuscript, and for some fact-checking. They also correct syntax, spelling, and punctuation.

COPY FITTING: Designing text to fit into a predetermined amount of space or number of pages. It results in the specification of **FONT** and **LEADING** (e.g., Helvetica 11/13, meaning 11-point Helvetica type set on 13 **POINTS** of space, a point being 1/72 of an inch).

COPYRIGHT: The exclusive legal right to reproduce, publish, sell, or distribute the matter and form of something such as a literary, musical, or artistic work. The extent of copyright protection and the enforcement of it differ among countries. For various reasons, it is wise to register copyrights with the Library of Congress, although that is not required. Book **FRONT MATTER** should include a copyright notice with the copyright symbol or the word *Copyright*, the year of first publication, and the name of the copyright holder. Book titles cannot be copyrighted. For current copyright law, see "Copyright Basics," *copyright.gov/circs/circ01.pdf*.

COVER ART: The design for a book's front, back, and **SPINE**, or for a **HARDCOVER**'s dust cover, aka jacket.

COVER STOCK: A heavier paper used for paperback covers. The terms for cover-stock specifications are different from the terms for text-stock specifications; a 50# text stock is not the same as the 50# cover stock sold in office supply stores for postcards. An example of a cover-stock *SPEC* is 10 pt. C1S, with 10 pt. being the weight and C1S being "coated one side."

CREATESPACE: The Amazon.com *PRINT-ON-DEMAND* service that produces books using digital printing.

CREEP: The distance margins shift when *SIGNATURES* are *FOLDED AND GATHERED* for insertion in a book's cover. The amount of creep will vary depending on both the number and the thickness of the sheets and must be compensated for during *LAYOUT* and *IMPOSITION*. Because *CHECK COPIES (F&GS)* and *BULKING DUMMIES* are hand-folded, they may not accurately represent creep.

CROP: To reduce the size or change the dimensions of an illustration by removing part of one or more sides rather than reducing the size of the entire image.

CROP MARKS: Lines on the *CAMERA-READY ART* that show where cuts will be made for the final *TRIM*. See also *BLEED*.

CROSS-REFERENCE: A term that refers the reader to related material within the same work.

CSR: Customer service representative. CSRs are sometimes employed by printers and publishers to replace salespeople as the liaison between the customer and the production staff, since they are in-house staff and can be more available for a customer's queries than salespeople. CSRs do not typically have production experience and so must consult printing or bindery staff on technical questions.

CTP: Computer-to-plate, the ***PREPRESS*** process used when everything is digital—that is, when pages are created and arranged on a computer and then made into a ***PRINTING PLATE***, which is what goes on the press to transfer the image to paper. By contrast, computer-to-film, the traditional process prior to digital files, requires that ***PASTEUPS*** (aka ***MECHANICALS)*** be photographed and the negative used to create the plate. Because CTP eliminates one reproduction step, it increases the quality of the reproduction, and there is no chance that negative film will be damaged by dust spots.

CURL: Distortions in pages because of excess moisture or humidity.

CUTTER DUST: Paper dust resulting from cutting or trimming the paper. It can transfer to ***PRINTING BLANKETS***, causing problems during a press run.

CYAN: ***PROCESS*** blue ink.

DAISY: Digital Accessible Information SYstem makes text accessible to people with visual or other difficulties in reading books. See DAISY, *daisy.org*.

DASH: A typographical line longer than a hyphen (which should not be used to create it). Short ones are en dashes; long ones are *EM* dashes.

DEBOSSING: The opposite of embossing, in which a die is pressed against paper to create raised type or a raised image. With debossing, the die creates depressed images.

DECORATION: A decorative character often used as part of a folio (i.e., page number) or to indicate transitions, such as those between sections or at the end of an article. Prior to *OFFSET* lithography, decorations provided small images without the expense of custom engraving.

Various traditional DECORATIONS

DEDICATION: An inscription by the author (and sometimes the illustrator and/or editor) that appears in the *FRONT MATTER*, usually following the *VERSO* (the reverse side of the title page) but sometimes on the top of the verso page.

DELIMITER: A character that is used to separate items of information, which is important when information is transferred from one format to another. A mailing service may ask that a mailing list be exported from a database in tab- or comma-delimited format.

DENSITY: The degree of darkness (blackness) of a photographic image.

DEPOSIT COPIES: The copies of a book sent with the completed *COPYRIGHT* application and fee to the Library of Congress. See "Mandatory Deposit," *copyright.gov/help/faq/mandatory_deposit.html.*

DESCENDER: That portion of a letter—the tails of lower-case *g*, *j*, and *p*, for example—that extends below the *BASELINE*. When type is *LEADED* too tightly, descenders and *ASCENDERS* can overlap.

DEVELOPMENTAL EDIT: Editing that deals with the content and quality of a manuscript, addressing organization, transitions, tone, voice, and complexity.

DIE-CUTTING: Cutting a shape out of paper, usually out of the cover of a paperback book. This bindery process can be done with standard dies that the printer or bindery has in stock (e.g., an oval shape) or with a custom die, such as a company logo, which increases costs. Dies are also required for *DEBOSSING* and *EMBOSSING*.

DIGITAL: Used to describe type and images that exist on computers rather than paper and are transferred electronically or with such storage devices as flash drives.

DIGITAL CONTENT AGGREGATOR: An online entity that gathers and disseminates digital content from a variety of sources.

DIGITAL OBJECT IDENTIFIER: Identifies intellectual property of any kind. Introduced by the International DOI Foundation, *doi.org*, to identify any entity—physical, digital, or abstract—primarily for sharing or managing as intellectual property (e.g., through licensing). DOIs also enable tracking owners of intellectual property such as a book or database.

DIGITAL RIGHTS MANAGEMENT (DRM): Encryption or coding of e-books and other digital publications to make it impossible (or at least difficult) to copy, save, download, or print the material. Some publishers want all material protected, which means an e-book can be read only on the device for which it is purchased; others have chosen to make their e-book content available for use on as many electronic devices as the customer chooses.

DIGITIZATION: The conversion of material from printed to digital format, often with a process such as *SCANNING*.

DINGBAT: A printing symbol such as a bullet, heart, box, or diamond. Most desktop publishing programs provide dingbats in the Zapf Dingbats *FONT*.

DIRECT MAIL (AKA DIRECT RESPONSE ADVERTISING): Promotional material snail-mailed to prospective customers. "Direct response" means it solicits immediate orders. Direct mail is usually sent at bulk rates, which are significantly lower than first-class postal rates, but require permits, indicia, presorting, and delivery to a bulk mail processing facility.

DISCOUNTS: In book wholesaling and retailing, the percentage deducted from a book's cover price. A *WHOLESALER* may pay $4.50 for a $10 book with a 55 percent wholesale discount and sell it to a bookseller at a 40 percent discount from cover price, or $6, grossing $1.50 in this example.

DISTRIBUTE AND PRINT/DISTRIBUTIVE PRINTING: The process of sending a file for a book to have it printed as close to the end user as possible. With digital printing, a U.S. publisher can have books printed by European partners at significant savings in time and freight cost.

DISTRIBUTOR: One of the possible intermediaries between a publisher and booksellers. In traditional publishing with books printed *OFFSET*, the distributor sells to book *WHOLESALERS* and retailers, purchasing books directly from the publisher at a discount from cover price, sometimes as much as 70 percent. Some distributors handle all sales except those explicitly retained by the publisher, such as sales in bulk to corporations. Distributors usually have sales reps who call on bookstore chains, large independent bookstores, and wholesalers. (Wholesalers typically do not have salespeople.) Some publisher-distributor relationships are exclusive. Relationships with distributors for special markets such as gift shops or health-food stores are often nonexclusive. Most large and many small publishers self-distribute to wholesalers and/or bookstores and/or libraries. For digital products, a vendor such as Amazon's *CREATESPACE* may be the distributor. E-book distributors include such companies as OverDrive and Smashwords.

DITCH: The space between columns of type on a page.

DITHERING: The process of varying a pattern of dots to create the illusion of colors that are not available with the printing process and inks being used. For example, with *CMYK*, dots of different red, cream, and white shades might create a pattern that makes the eye think it is seeing pink. *HALFTONES*, the reproducible images of black-and-white photos, are produced with dithering; the pattern of interspersed black and white dots creates the illusion of different grays.

DOT GAIN: When ink spreads past the specified dot size and thus makes tones darker or colors stronger. Dot gain can also make images look muddy or blurred. It affects highly absorbent papers such as newsprint more than hard, coated stock, which is why paper should be specified before *SCREENING* is selected for an image. A photo to be printed on newsprint should be prepared with a coarser line screen (fewer *LINES PER INCH*; or lower lpi) and thus fewer dots per inch to compensate for dot gain.

DOTS PER INCH (DPI): A measurement of the resolution of a laser or inkjet printer. A higher dpi yields crisper images and type. Sources differ on how dpi compares to *LINES PER INCH* (lpi): some printers and designers recommend that images be created as *TIFFs* with dpi at least double the lpi that will be used when a *HALFTONE* is made for printing. Following this recommendation, a photo would be created at no less than 600 dpi if it were to be screened at 300 lpi. Other sources recommend a much greater difference: 600 dpi for an image to be used in a newspaper, which may have an 85-line screen (lpi); or 2400 dpi for an image that will appear in a glossy magazine, which may have a 150-to 200-line screen (lpi).

DOUBLE BUMP: To print twice so a page has two layers of the same color ink, which may be necessary because the stock (usually a cover) is heavily textured and requires two applications for good coverage. Images printed with a double bump have an extra-rich, or deep, color.

DOUBLETRUCK: Two facing pages of a publication used for an image, usually an advertisement.

DRILLING: The print industry term for punching holes, as for pages to be inserted in ring binders.

DROP CAP: An oversized initial capital sometimes used at the beginning of a magazine story or book chapter. It will be the height of several lines of type.

DROP FOLIO: A page number printed at the bottom of the page.

DROP SHIP: Shipping of products such as books directly from the manufacturer to a *WHOLESALER*, *DISTRIBUTOR*, retailer, or end user. A publisher that uses an exclusive distributor will probably have almost all its inventory shipped directly to the distributor's warehouse. A publisher that has received significant advance orders for a title (say, quantities of 1,000 or more) may have those orders fulfilled via drop shipping. Drop shipping usually increases the freight costs from the point of manufacture but reduces the labor and cost for fulfilling large orders from the publisher's warehouse. (With drop shipping, the publisher may not see the finished book before fulfillment of orders has begun. This means that if an error occurs after the publisher has reviewed the *LASER PROOFS*, *BLUELINES*, or *FOLDED AND GATHERED SHEETS [F&GS]*, poor-quality copies may be received by retailers before the publisher is aware of the problem.) Many

POD vendors now ship directly from the printing plant to retail customers who have ordered online.

DUMMY: A stand-in for the finished book. A folding dummy is compiled of blank pages of specified cover stock and text stock, usually to determine spine width (for the purpose of creating spine artwork), and possibly also to determine weight (for estimating freight costs) and number of copies per carton (when discounts are based on full-carton sales). Sometimes pages are dummied with actual text to determine space available for photos and photo placement.

DUMP BIN: A floor display, often a self-contained shipping carton that is assembled as a display unit for paperback books or sidelines (nonbook products such as notecards, toys, or jewelry). Publishers that offer dump bins describe them, and the number of books included, in their trade catalogs and/or on their websites. The counter prepack is a smaller version of a dump bin.

DUOTONE: A two-color *HALFTONE*. Often used for special effects or when the budget does not permit full-color images. Technically, a halftone (grayscale image) with a second color overlaid on a portion of the image.

DUST JACKET: The paper or acetate cover folded over a bound book, usually a *HARDCOVER*. Also called a dust cover, a book jacket, or simply a jacket, it usually includes more graphics, promotional text, and author biographical information than the cover accommodates. Publishers that order extra copies of the dust jacket can often use them to replace damaged dust jackets on books returned from retailers, allowing those books to be resold as new.

EAN, EUROPEAN ARTICLE NUMBER: EANs are 13-digit identifiers assigned to all kinds of products available for retail sale worldwide. The 13-digit ISBNs now used on books are part of the larger EAN system.

EARLY READERS: Beginning *CHAPTER BOOKS* usually oriented to children ages 8–11 who are advancing to them from picture books; typically 64 pages long and generously illustrated, often in black and white.

EARN OUT: When a book has sold enough copies so that *ROYALTIES* due equal the amount of the author's *ADVANCE*, the advance is said to have "earned out."

E-BLAST: The mass distribution of an email message, usually through an email marketing service (for examples of vendors, see the Email Sender and Provider Coalition website, espcoalition.org/members.list).

E-BOOK: A book published in *DIGITAL* form and usually accessible via a computer, a Kindle, NOOK, iPad, smartphone, tablet, or other handheld device.

E-BOOK FORMATS: EPub and Mobi are two of the most common formats for e-books. EPub is open format and supported by Apple's iBooks, the Nook, and most other e-Readers. Mobi is now owned by Amazon. The first commonly used cross-platform format was *PDF*, still commonly used for government documents and short publications sold directly from a publisher's website.

EDITION: The paperback reprint of a hardcover title is technically the same edition, but each version requires a different *ISBN*; in general, different versions are referred to as editions—e.g., "trade paper edition," "mass market edition," "movie tie-in edition." A version with significant revisions is considered a new edition. Editions can be numbered (e.g., "Second Edition") or described (e.g., "Revised").

EDITOR: In a large publishing company, editorial responsibilities are divided among such positions as *ACQUISITIONS EDITOR*, *DEVELOPMENTAL EDITOR*, *COPY EDITOR*, production editor, and technical editor. In smaller publishing companies, one person called simply "editor" may fulfill several editorial roles. In some publishing companies, a "production editor" coordinates and traffics the editorial side of the production process; in others, this is the job of the "production director" or "production manager." *Editor* is also the word used to describe the person who assembles content for an anthology.

ELECTRONIC DATA INTERCHANGE (EDI): EDI refers to standards for electronic transactions that allow automated ordering. For example, after a publisher places a print order from its inventory system, the publisher-generated purchase order and specifications are uploaded to the print vendor's system, which then sends a shipping confirmation to the publisher and eventually sends the publisher a bill.

ELHI: The abbreviation for the elementary and secondary school markets and for texts and other materials produced for those markets.

EM: An American unit of measure in typesetting. The em of a particular *FACE* is as wide as its capital letter *M* and as deep as its *POINT* size (e.g., in 10-point type text, an em bullet will be the width of the upper case *M* and 10 points high). Because some type styles are *CONDENSED* and some are *EXPANDED*, the size of an em varies from font to font even within the same point size. Dashes are often specified as "em" or "en," with en being half the width of em.

EMBOSSED: Printed or stamped with a design or type created from a die (see *DIE-CUTTING* regarding standard and custom dies). The design or type may be blank, covered with *FOIL*, or printed.

ENAMEL: A form of *COATED* paper.

END MATTER: Also known as *BACK MATTER*; the material following the text of a book. For example, appendices, *END-NOTES*, glossaries, and indexes.

ENDNOTE: With the same content as footnotes, endnotes appear at the end of a chapter or in *END MATTER*.

EOM: End of the month, a financial term referring to when payments are scheduled. *WHOLESALERS* typically pay 60 or 90 days after the end of the month in which they shipped books to retailers, which may be several months after they received the books from the publisher.

EPIGRAPH: A quotation at the beginning of a book or chapter intended to convey an idea that will be developed in the text.

EPILOGUE: Usually a brief summary of what occurred after the plot or action in a book. Sometimes epilogues are added to successive *EDITIONS* of a nonfiction book to update the content of the original. Part of the *END MATTER*.

EPS: Encapsulated PostScript, a common file format for exporting Adobe Illustrator files. It uses *POSTSCRIPT* coding and so can be output to a PostScript printer, but it cannot be used instead of a *JPEG* or *TIFF* image for printing.

E-PUB and EPUB: *E-pub* is a generic term broader than *e-book* that also describes periodicals delivered as digital publications. EPUB is the standard for representing, packaging, and encoding structured and semantically enhanced web content—including XHTML, CSS, SVG, images, and other resources—for distribution in a single-file format. The current version is EPUB 3; detailed information is available from the International Digital Publishing Forum, *idpf.org*.

E-READER: A handheld digital device—Kindle, iPad, or NOOK, for example—onto which electronic publications can be downloaded. Most e-readers require reformatting of text originally prepared for print.

EROTIC ROMANCE: Fiction with sex as an important element in a plot that includes the conflict and resolution typical of romance fiction.

EROTICA: Fiction with sex as the major plot activity. Similar to soft porn.

ERRATA: The common name for the sheet slipped into or pasted into a book noting corrections of errors found after the book was printed.

ESCALATION (OR ESCALATOR) CLAUSE: In an author's contract with a publisher, this clause defines what entitles the author to additional or increased ***ROYALTY*** payments. For example, the royalty rate may be 5 percent of the cover price on the first 5,000 copies sold, and escalate to 7.5 percent on the second 5,000 copies and to 10 percent on all sales in excess of 10,000.

ESPRESSNET: The online database of book texts available for printing on Espresso Book Machines.

ESPRESSO BOOK MACHINE: The EBM is one of several recently introduced point-of-purchase "kiosks" that can print, bind, and trim a book while a customer waits. See On Demand Books, *ondemandbooks.com*.

EVERGREEN: A publication that is considered to always be in demand and thus is never allowed to go out of print; e.g., a classic.

EXAMINATION COPY: A copy sent on approval or at no charge to a prospective customer, usually an educator considering a book for a course. Some publishers specify that the recipient will be billed for the book if it is not adopted for the course and not returned within 30 days. Also called an inspection copy.

EXCERPT: Material from a larger source. When an excerpt appears in a book, it is usually set off with indenting. On the ***VERSO*** page of a book, a publisher often specifies that only

The Language of Publishing

brief excerpts of the book can be reprinted and only in reviews unless written permission is granted by the *COPYRIGHT* holder. Authors and publishers often excerpt material from their books for use in articles and posts.

An EXPANDED FACE has wider characters than its "regular" or "normal" counterpart.

EXPANDED FACE: A *FONT* with especially wide characters, usually more rounded and often with heavier stroke. Expanded faces are often used for titles or chapter headings, and in advertising. Desktop publishing programs such as InDesign allow type to be increased in width and extra space to be added between characters to create the impression of an expanded face.

4-0-0-4: A printing specification that indicates a book cover is to be printed in four colors on the front and back with no printing on the inside of the front and back covers. 4-1-1-4 means four colors on the front and back with one color (usually black) on the inside front and back covers. Digital presses typically produce covers 4-0-0-4.

FACE: Traditionally, a type style, such as Bodoni, Arial, or Times Roman. Now more commonly used to refer to a given style of a *FONT* (e.g., Bodoni italic, Bodoni book, Bodoni bold).

FACSIMILE EDITION: An exact reproduction of an original (usually vintage) work, today made by *SCANNING* the pages of the original, which often requires removing the binding. A facsimile edition will show any errors on the original printed pages.

FACT-CHECKING: Reviewing material presented as fact in a manuscript to verify its accuracy. For fiction, fact-checking may involve researching the historical accuracy of such story elements as places, events, modes of transportation, and available technology. For nonfiction, it may include verifying quotations. Today fact-checking also may entail confirming that URLs are cited correctly. Authors are often primarily responsible for checking facts, although *EDITORS* and *COPYEDITORS* may do some fact-checking.

FAIR USE: Often claimed when *COPYRIGHTED* material is used without authorization from the copyright holder, *fair use* is a legal term. Whether a use is legally "fair" is determined by considering four factors: the purpose and character of the use, including whether it is of a commercial nature or is for non-profit educational purposes; the nature of the copyrighted work; the amount and substantiality of the portion used in relation to the copyrighted work as a whole; and the effect of the use on the potential market for or value of the copyrighted work. The verso page of a book sometimes explains how much of the text can be excerpted and for what purpose without obtaining the copyright holder's authorization.

FAMILY, FONT, or TYPE: See *FONT*.

FANTASY: A genre often linked with science fiction. Characters in fantasy include anthropomorphized animals and objects (talking cars, say), aliens, humanoids, robots, dwarves, elves, goblins, and vampires.

FICTION: A literary genre with characters and/or plot lines created by the author, and therefore not basically factual.

FILE TRANSFER PROTOCOL (FTP): A common means of exchanging electronic files, usually such large ones as book files, over the Internet from one computer to another or from one server to another. For receipt of files, most printers and book manufacturers have FTP portals with specific addresses and passwords.

FILM: In traditional *OFFSET* printing, a *MECHANICAL* (*COMPS*, *PASTEUP*) was photographed, and the film—actually the film negative—was used to create printing plates.

Every dust spot or scratch on a negative would create a spot on the printed page, so negatives were proofed on a light table and defects were "opaqued" out with a special masking fluid.

FILM LAMINATION: Bonding plastic film to paper, usually *COVER STOCK*, to protect the paper and improve its appearance.

FINISHED SIZE: The final size of a book after *BINDING* and trimming. Similar to *TRIM SIZE*, which specifies the height and width.

FINISHING: Specialty *BINDING* operations such as *DIE-CUTTING*, hand-gluing, inserting CDs, and *SHRINK-WRAPPING*—everything that occurs after the book is printed.

FIRST SERIAL RIGHTS: The legal right to publish a forthcoming book in installments or to publish an *EXCERPT* from it in a periodical. Magazine and newspaper publishers may pay for first serial rights for major titles. For other titles, publicists offer free serial rights to generate interest in the book either before publication (first serial) or after (second serial).

FLAP COPY: Promotional text that appears on the front and back flaps of the *DUST JACKET* of a *HARDCOVER* book. On a paperback, similar promotional text may appear on the inside front cover and/or on the back cover.

FLAT: The large sheet to which *OFFSET* negatives or positives are physically attached for the production of an offset printing plate. With *DIGITAL* or computer-to-plate technology, it is no longer used.

FLAT FEE: One-time compensation for a writer, illustrator, or photographer in lieu of royalties.

FLUORESCENT INKS: Inks that add radiance. More expensive than regular *PANTONE MATCHING SYSTEMS® (PMS®)* colors and more likely to fade, they may require a second pass (aka *DOUBLE BUMP*) for adequate coverage.

FLUSH: Even with. Flush left means that type is set block style with all lines except paragraph indents even with the left margin. Flush right, occasionally used for titles and display type, means the right side of a text block aligns with the right margin.

FLYLEAF: A blank page in the front of a book. Part of the *FRONT MATTER*.

FOB: Freight on board, free on board. Refers to where goods will be delivered without freight charges. If the book manufacturer's quote specifies FOB Ann Arbor, the publisher will pay for delivery from Ann Arbor, MI.

FOIL: Tissue-thin material with metal or pigment that is pressed onto the cover of a book with a heated die. See also *EMBOSSING*).

FOLDED AND GATHERED SHEETS (F&GS): Printed *SIGNATURES* of a book that have been *COLLATED* but not yet glued or bound. They are used sometimes for *PROOFREADING* and sometimes for prepublication promotion.

FOLDING: In *OFFSET* printing, *BOOK BLOCKS* are produced in *SIGNATURES*, with the number of pages always a multiple of eight. Children's picture books, for example, are usually created in 32-page signatures, which means that each sheet coming off the press has 16 pages on each side. The sheet is folded to create the pages in sequence. Most folding of book signatures is done on the press, or inline. ***CHECK COPIES*** of ***DUST JACKETS*** may be hand folded, and may misrepresent the accuracy available with machine-folded jackets; to ensure that a book's dust jacket artwork will be the exact size needed, ask the book manufacturer for the exact spine width, and for a ***HARDCOVER*** ask whether the spine will be flat or curved. When changing book manufacturers for a subsequent edition, determine the spine width and style before submitting dust cover artwork.

FOLIO: The numeral in a paginated book, including any artwork used with the numeral; also, the number on a right-hand page.

FONT: The complete set of characters, including numbers, punctuation, and bullets, in a given ***TYPEFACE***. Traditionally each font included one size and one style; for example, 24-point Times Italic. All the sizes and styles were called a font (or type) family, with typeface variations usually including roman (regular), bold, and italic; light, semibold, bold italic, book, black, and extra-bold; ***CONDENSED*** and ***EXPANDED*** faces could also be included. Today style is usually denoted by a "face" such as bold or italic. When a print job is submitted in ***NATIVE*** or ***POSTSCRIPT*** files, all the fonts used in the publication must be submitted to the book manufacturer, including ***DINGBATS***, ***DECORATIONS***, and symbols. (In desktop publishing some of these will be in the "glyphs" file.) A job submitted as a ***PDF*** does not require submission of fonts.

FONT METRICS: The spacing attributes of type. This is part of the reason that a font on one computer is unlikely to match the font of the same name (e.g., Times Roman) on another computer, unless both were loaded from the same release of the same software, and it is why an electronic file must be accompanied by its fonts when sent to the printer unless submitted as a *PDF*.

FONT SIZE: The size (height) of a character in a particular *FONT* as measured in *POINTS* from the lowest *DESCENDER* to the highest *ASCENDER*. Because there are 72 points to an inch, a character in 36-point type is theoretically a half-inch high—but no single character has both an ascender and descender.

FOOT: The bottom of a page.

FOOTNOTE: A note at the bottom of a page, usually a reference, authority, translation, or explanation of text appearing on the same page. The information in footnotes can appear instead in *ENDNOTES* at the end of each chapter or in a book's *END MATTER*.

FOREIGN RIGHTS: The rights to publish a book, either in its original language or in translation, outside the country of origin. Foreign rights may be limited to a specific language in a specific geographic area: for example, Mandarin Chinese in China, or Spanish in Mexico (but not South America or Spain). Given the number of languages and countries in the world today, agents and publishers can make many foreign rights sales for a single book, and, since foreign rights are usually sold for a specified number of years, they can sometimes resell rights.

FOREWORD: An introductory section of a book written by someone other than the author. Part of the *FRONT MATTER*.

FOUR-COLOR PRINTING, FOUR-COLOR PROCESS: Creating full-color material during the printing process with the four process ink colors cyan, magenta, yellow, and black (*CMYK*). *OFFSET* printing requires a *SEPARATION* and plate for each of the four.

FPO: For position only. Used to identify proxy images in a layout, often so that text can be paginated prior to the acquisition of the actual images.

FRENCH FOLD: A sheet, usually oversize, printed on one side and folded into quarters to be *TIPPED* in (bound into a book). The fold along the top edge is not cut, so that the sheet is whole when unfolded by a reader. Used with oversize images such as maps or pedigrees.

FRICTIONLESS FILE CONVERSION: A highly scalable conversion process for transforming PDFs, native files, or physical books into *POD* print-ready files.

FRONT MATTER: The first pages of a book preceding the text, sometimes not numbered; sometimes numbered with lowercase Roman numerals. Front matter can include (in the traditional order) the *HALF TITLE*, a list of books by the same author or in the same series, a *FRONTISPIECE*, a title page, a *COPYRIGHT* page (*VERSO*), a *DEDICATION*, a table of contents, a list of illustrations, a *FOREWORD*, a *PREFACE*, an introduction, and a second half title. Today few trade titles include all of these, and front matter elements are often combined on a few pages. For example, the dedication may appear on the copyright (verso) page.

FRONTISPIECE: An illustration facing the title page. In books produced by *LETTERPRESS*, the frontispiece was often the only illustration, or the only color illustration.

FRONTLIST: A publisher's new books. Many large publishers issue books twice annually, and the spring list will be considered frontlist until the fall titles are introduced. At that point the spring titles become *BACKLIST*. Smaller publishers may consider titles frontlist for a longer period and consider backlist *EVERGREEN*.

FTP: *FILE TRANSFER PROTOCOL*.

FULFILLMENT: The processes included in shipping and billing books to a customer. Often also called order fulfillment in business in general. *DISTRIBUTORS* that sell books on an exclusive basis for their client publishers usually also handle fulfillment for them. Some publishers outsource fulfillment to fulfillment houses or warehousing services, which receive and store books, process the purchase orders sent by the publisher, pack and ship books, and receive and process returns.

GALLEYS, GALLEY PROOFS: Originally, a galley was the long, narrow tray in which metal type stood after being set, either by hand or with a hot-lead typesetter such as a Linotype. Galley proofs were the long sheets of paper with impressions made from the type in the trays. Today galley proofs might consist of unpaginated text, but more commonly they're page proofs (see also *ARC*s). Initial *PAGE PROOFS*, used for *PROOFREADING*, may have no images or have only blocks reserved for images.

GAMUT: A complete subset of colors. When certain colors cannot be displayed within a particular color model, those colors are said to be out of gamut. For example, the pure red in the *RGB* color model gamut is out of gamut in the *CMYK* model and an approximation must be created.

GANGING: When related jobs using the same paper and ink are grouped together on a printing plate and thus on the press. For example, a book manufacturer might gang covers with postcards that use *COVER ART* to be printed together and cut apart after printing. Before electronic prepress, color photographs were sometimes ganged for *SEPARATION* to reduce costs. This had the disadvantage of reducing quality, because colors and contrast could not be adjusted for individual photos.

GATEFOLD: Technically, a wide sheet with foldouts on either side of the *CENTER SPREAD*. The term is also used for an extra-wide page that has one foldout. Covers sometimes have a gatefold (commonly on magazines that sell the inside cover for advertising). A gatefold may also be used to accommodate an extra-wide image such as a map, chart, or photograph. A gatefold text page must be *TIPPED* in—that is, added during *OFFLINE BINDING*. Gatefolds are not available with *DIGITAL* printing.

GATHERING: *COLLATING* printed pages in consecutive order. In book production, pages are often folded and gathered on a press. When the press can produce only a small number of pages at one time, *SIGNATURES* or groups of signatures are gathered offline as a final step.

GENERATION: Each successive version of an image, and sometimes of type. With traditional *OFFSET* printing, the comprehensive is the original, the negative the second generation, and the plate the third. This means the printed copy is at least the fourth generation. With a photograph made from film, the original print would have been reproduced even more times before it appeared in a book. The *FACSIMILE* of a book text, usually made by *SCANNING* printed pages as images, is at least the fifth generation. With direct-to-plate printing, the number of generations is reduced, the opportunity for error is reduced, and the quality of the type and images should be better.

GENRE PUBLISHING: Also category publishing. Genres include self-help, mystery, romance, history, and many more.

GHOSTING: Unwanted images on the printed piece that should be corrected after a *PRESS CHECK*.

GHOSTWRITER: Someone who writes a work that will be credited to someone else as the author. A ghost may create a manuscript in part or in whole, often on a ***WORK-FOR-HIRE*** basis. Ghostwriters are sometimes acknowledged with language such as "as told to" or "with" or by having their names included in lists of contributors or in acknowledgments sections. Some ghosts also write under their own names.

GIF, GRAPHICS INTERCHANGE FORMAT: A bitmap image format introduced by CompuServe that can be used on websites but lacks the quality necessary for printing.

GIGABYTE: A unit of electronic storage; equal to 1,024 megabytes.

GLOSSARY: A dictionary of terms relevant to a book's content, found in the ***END MATTER***.

GLOSS INK: Ink with an extra quantity of varnish, which produces a shiny appearance when dry.

GLOSS, GLOSSY, GLOSSIE PRINT: Gloss is a finish available on paper and with ***COATINGS*** such as varnishes (contrast with ***MATTE*** or ***FLAT***). Glossy prints are photographs made on shiny paper. Photographs printed for reproduction are usually glossies.

GRAIN: The way fibers align in paper stock. Grain long means a paper's grain runs parallel to the longer measurement of a sheet of the paper—that is, the fibers align with the length of the sheet. Grain short is the opposite—the paper's grain runs at right angles to the longer dimension of the paper sheet. Paper will curl, fold, and tear more easily in the direction of its grain. To check grain, bend a sheet without creating a fold, or spray water on one side; the paper will curl with the grain.

When publications are printed cross-grain to save money (because more signatures can sometimes then fit on a plate), the bound materials are often called "mouse traps" because they give the publication a tendency to close.

GRAININESS: Print quality characterized by unevenness, particularly of *HALFTONES*.

GRAPHICS: Visual material, as opposed to text, including photographs, drawings, paintings, and charts. Also see *IMAGES*.

GRAVURE: Intaglio printing, now seen primarily in photographic books and *FRONTISPIECES*. Distinguished by dense solids and (in *HALFTONES*) an almost invisible *SCREEN*. The roll-fed process by which large-circulation photo magazines and newspapers, Sunday magazines were often produced is called rotogravure.

GRAYSCALE: *HALFTONES* are grayscale images, usually photos with as many as 256 shades of gray. Color images are often converted to grayscale for reproduction in books, especially paperbacks.

GREEKED TEXT: Meaningless blocks of characters that are used to mock up layouts during the design process. When pages in a desktop publishing program are reduced significantly in size so that the type becomes too small to be legible, it's said to be greeked.

GREEKED TEXT is meaningless blocks of characters often used in mockups.

GRID: An x-y layout of lines for typographic *PASTEUPS*, to enable accurate alignment of images and columns of type. With phototypesetting for *OFFSET* production, pale blue grids were printed on cover stock cut slightly larger than each page or spread. Galleys were waxed on their reverse sides and positioned using the gridlines.

GRIPPER, GRIPPER MARGIN: On a sheet-fed press, grippers clamp the paper and control its movement. The gripper margin is the narrow space where the paper is clamped and no ink can be laid. For a book cover or page to have a *BLEED* image, the sheet must be trimmed inside the gripper margin. This wastes paper and is one reason bleeds typically increase the cost of a printing job.

GROUNDWOOD PULP: The material from which newsprint and similar papers are made, which lacks permanence because it turns brittle quickly. It is often used not only in newspapers but also in mass market paperbacks and such inexpensive children's publications as coloring books.

GUIDE MARKS: The crossline marks on an *OFFSET LITHO-GRAPHY* press plate that indicate *TRIM*, centering of the sheet, centering of the plate, and so on; also called *REGISTER MARKS*.

GUILLOTINE: The device that trims stacks of paper to the desired size.

GUTTER: Inside margins on a page come together to create the gutter. Except on the *CENTER SPREAD* of a *SIGNATURE*, the gutter can have no printing.

HAIRLINE: A thin printed stroke, or in the case of a hairline rule, a thin printed line.

HAIRLINE REGISTER: The term used in *OFFSET* printing when two or more colors are aligned to within a hairline—that is, within the space of less than half a row of *HALFTONE* dots.

HALF TITLE: The page facing the title page with the book title on it. A traditional part of the *FRONT MATTER*.

A close-up of dots that make up a HALFTONE.

HALFTONE: An image such as a black-and-white photograph that is converted for printing in one color with a line screen that breaks the photograph's continuous spectrum of blacks, whites, and grays into black dots and white dots. A higher concentration of black dots results in a darker shade. Images that are **SCREENED** and then printed in two colors are **DUOTONES**.

HANGING INDENTION: A typesetting format in which the first line is set flush to the left margin and the following lines are indented. Often seen in dictionaries.

HARDCOVER: Hardcover (or "hardbound") books are made when the cover is glued to a cloth-covered book board. Typically the title, author, and publisher names are stamped on the **SPINE**. **DUST JACKETS** are common for hardcover trade books. A classic hardcover book is called **CASEBOUND**, and the **BOOK BLOCK** is trimmed before the cover is bound to it.

HARD RETURN: In word processing or desktop publishing, the equivalent of a carriage return, a manual keystroke that ends the current line and starts a new paragraph. Hard returns should not be used within paragraphs of book text. Creating them in **HTML** requires a tag.

HEAD: The top of the page, or the title or headline of a written work.

HEADER: Running heads, or headers, are the lines of type that run above the text, usually in proximity to page numbers. In books, the running head on left-hand pages may supply the title of the book and the running head on right-hand pages may supply the title of the chapter or the name of the author. Other arrangements are normal too, and some designers put this sort of information at the bottoms of pages, creating a "running foot" or "footer" for each.

HEAT-SET INKS: Used in high-speed web offset printing, these set rapidly under heat and are quickly chilled.

HICKEY: Spots or other imperfections on the printed page due to dirt or debris on the *OFFSET* press.

HIGH BULK: Book paper manufactured with a thickness greater than other papers of the same basis weight. Frequently used to give thickness to a book with a minimal number of pages.

HIGH RESOLUTION: An image is "high res" when it is reproduced with quality high enough to show a significant amount of detail or with a high level of gray scaling. High-resolution images take up more electronic space, so it takes more time to send them via email or load them on a website. That's why websites use *JPEG*s, which are typically lower resolution than *TIFF*s. Converting a JPEG to a TIFF can be done, but it will not improve its resolution. In printing, the higher the *DPI* or line screen used to create an image, the higher the resolution it can have. Partly because of the amount of memory high-resolution images require, book manuscripts with images are often transferred from publisher to printer via *FTP*.

HI-LO BOOKS: Written for those who read at a level lower than expected for their age, these books use simple language and sentence construction to provide information for middle graders to adults.

HOT TYPE, HOT METAL: Type created from melted lead for use by equipment such as the Linotype machine, now largely replaced by phototypesetting equipment, although hot type may still be used with *LETTERPRESS* printing.

HOUSE STOCK: Book papers that a book manufacturer inventories in large quantities, which are therefore less expensive than paper the book manufacturer must order just for a specific job.

HTML: HyperText Markup Language, used for coding, or tagging, text for websites. HTML is not a computer language. Right-clicking with a mouse (on a PC) and selecting "view page source" makes HTML code visible.

HURTS: Damaged or shopworn books, also called scuffs and seconds. These may be books damaged in shipping, or damaged copies returned from a retailer, *WHOLESALER*, or exhibit. Typically, they cannot be sold to a wholesaler, so publishers often sell them direct at a reduced price.

ILLO: Illustration.

IMAGES: Drawings, photographs, or other graphics. For print production, these are best prepared as *TIFF*s. If a job is submitted in an electronic format other than *PDF*, the images must be submitted separately, and they must be electronically linked to the job's desktop publishing files for publication. Printers say that missing links are among the most common problems with electronic files. Software like *INDESIGN* allows links to be checked prior to submission of a job.

IMAGESETTER: A *HIGH-RESOLUTION* laser device that outputs to photosensitive paper or film.

IMITATION PARCHMENT: Paper made with irregular distribution of fibers.

IMPOSITION: The process of arranging images of individual pages so that they will be in the proper order after they are printed, folded, and trimmed. Imposition is an important step when books are printed in *SIGNATURES*, as in *OFFSET LITHOGRAPHY* or with digital web presses. In digital imaging, the imagesetter capable of outputting a film flat with four, eight, or more pages in imposed position is called an imposetter.

IMPRINT: As a noun, the name given to a publisher's line of books that has its own distinct characteristics. A publisher may choose to use imprint names to distinguish its mass market romances from its Christian fiction, or its trade fiction from its hardcover business titles, for example. As a verb, the process of printing other information on a previously printed piece by running it through a press again; for instance, a promotional message to postcards purchased from the U.S. Postal Service with preprinted postage.

INDESIGN: A commonly used Adobe Inc. desktop publishing program.

INDEX: An alphabetical list of topics in a book, with page references. Almost always used for nonfiction, an index is part of the ***END MATTER*** and important in marketing nonfiction to libraries.

INDEX.HTML: The home page of a website often has an extension using "index," e.g., *www.ibpa-online.org/index.aspx*.

INDICIA: Postal permit number and type, placed where a stamp would be. Ordinarily used for bulk mail, or ***DIRECT MAIL***. See "Permit Imprints," *pe.usps.com/text/qsg300/Q604d.htm*.

INDIE, INDEPENDENT BOOKSELLER: A single retail bookstore, or a bookstore with a few nearby branches. The Portland-based Powell's is considered an indie, although it has several outlets; Barnes & Noble and Books-a-Million, by contrast, are chains. Indie is sometimes also used to describe other independent businesses, including publishing companies.

INGRAMSPARK: A publisher services program introduced in 2013 oriented to smaller publishers than those served by Ingram's Lightning Source.

INK DOT SCUM: The problem that can result when oxidation occurs on aluminum printing plates, creating scattered pits that print sharp, dense dots.

INKJET PRINTING: The plateless system used in digital printing that produces images on paper from digital data. The images result from streams of very fine drops of dyes controlled by digital signals.

INLINE: Describes a production process or equipment that completes most or all manufacturing of a book or other printed piece in one operation.

INLINE BINDING: Available only for paperbacks, inline binding involves a print engine that feeds a *BOOK BLOCK* directly to a binding unit, a three-knife trimmer, and then a packing and boxing station. See *BINDING*.

INSERT: A printed piece prepared for insertion in a publication or other printed material.

INSIDE COVERS: The reverse side of the front cover is called simply the inside front cover, and the reverse of the back cover is called the inside back cover. On mass market titles, inside covers are often printed in black ink. Inside cover printing is not always available with digital presses See *4-0-0-4*.

INSTABOOK MAKER: This is one of the *POD* manufacturing devices that can be used in a point-of-purchase application. See *instabook.net*.

INSTITUTIONAL SALES: Sales to libraries and educational institutions, sometimes through trade channels, and sometimes direct from the publisher or through specialized outlets or ***DISTRIBUTORS***.

INTERLEAVES: Paper inserted between sheets as they come off the printing press to prevent transfer of wet ink from one page to another. Also called slip sheets.

ISBN: International Standard Book Number, the identifier for a particular title, printed on the ***COPYRIGHT*** page (***VERSO***) and on the back of the book. ***WHOLESALERS*** and ***DISTRIBUTORS*** require that books have ISBNs. So do almost all libraries and bookstores. Books printed before the late 1960s do not have ISBNs because the system was not created until then. ISBNs are available from R. R. Bowker. See *isbn.org/standards/home/index.asp*.

ISSN: International Standard Serial Number, used to identify magazines and other periodical publications just as the ***ISBN*** is used on books.

ITALIC: Type that slopes. There are true italic ***FACES***, and with desktop publishing software, roman (regular) type can be inclined to simulate italic. Book titles ordinarily appear in italic in typeset text.

JPEG: Joint Photographic Experts Group, the graphic file format created by digital cameras and used on websites. A JPEG (or JPG) does not offer the same potential for resolution as a *TIFF*, and so is not recommended for printed work. JPEGs can be converted to TIFFs, but the conversion will not improve the resolution.

JUSTIFY: Type with spacing adjusted between words so that each line is flush, or aligned, with both left and right margins is justified. In contrast, some type is *FLUSH* left and ragged right.

JUST-IN-TIME: An inventory strategy that can improve a business's return on investment by reducing inventory of raw materials and materials used in processing, along with their associated carrying costs. In publishing, the term refers to printing one copy or a few copies as orders arrive, or to printing a short run immediately after an order for, say, 100 copies is received. *POD, PRINT-ON-DEMAND*, is an example of just-in-time manufacturing.

Type with its spacing adjusted between words so that each line is flush, or aligned, both left and right is called justified.

Type that is flush left and ragged right is aligned on the left only.

JUSTIFIED text (top) vs. FLUSH left (bottom)

KERNING: Adjusting the space between letters. One of the major differences between typewritten text and typeset text is the kerning, how the letters fit together. "WA," for example, has less space between the letters when typeset than when typewritten. Such desktop publishing programs as InDesign allow letters to be kerned, even to the extreme that parts of one letter overlap parts of adjacent letters.

WAX	WAX	WAX
YOU	YOU	YOU
Two Words	Two Words	TwoWords

Typeset with no special kerning (left) vs. custom KERNING (center) vs. extremely tight kerning (right). Note the spaces between W and A, Y and O, and in-between words.

KEYWORDS: Online spiders—the software that indexes website text for search engines—often find relevant sites using the keywords site authors have entered near the beginning. The keywords on former IBPA President Florrie Binford Kichler's website for Patria Press include names specific to Patria's titles: "amelia earhart, william henry harrison, ben hur, lew wallace, james whitcomb riley, juliette low, eddie rickenbacker, mahalia jackson, george rogers clark, john hancock, phillis wheatley, abner doubleday."

KILL FEE: Some publisher-author contracts provide for the author to receive some payment if a manuscript is never published. The practice is more common with magazine contracts.

KNOCKOUT: To ensure that colors are reproduced accurately when multiple inks are used on a print job, *COLOR SEPARATIONS* may have areas blocked, or knocked out, so that they will not be covered with ink. Portions that are knocked out may appear in the color of the *COVER STOCK*. Knockouts are important because they prevent the color of a final ink such as a pastel from being distorted by an earlier bright or dark color.

LAMINATED: When a thin plastic film is applied to the outside cover of a book to protect the surface (say, from fingerprints or moisture) and enhance the appearance. Also see ***COATING***.

LARGE PRINT: Usually 18-or 20-***POINT*** type, large enough for comfortable use by some readers with visual impairments. Information about preparing materials for the visually impaired is available in "Best Practices and Guidelines for Large Print Documents Used by the Low Vision Community," provided by the Council of Citizens with Low Vision International, an affiliate of the American Council of the Blind.

LASER PRINTING: Typically done by a desktop printer that, like a photocopy machine, uses an electrostatically charged drum and toner to produce an image on paper. Contrast with ***OFFSET LITHOGRAPHY***, which involves transferring ink in a press from a printing ***PLATE*** to a rubber blanket to paper—a process with more expensive ***MAKE-READY*** and press cleanup that is suitable for longer runs.

LASER PROOFS: Paper output from an electronic file; used as final proof before printing. Also see ***BLUELINES***.

LAYFLAT BINDING: The process creates a flexible ***SPINE*** so pages lie flat when a book is open; popular for cookbooks and how-to books, when directions are likely to be read as a project is in process. Brands include Otabind and Repkover.

LAYOUT: The depiction of a design (as in "laying out the cover"). Also, what desktop publishing software creates as an electronic substitute for the *COMPREHENSIVE*, or *PASTEUP*.

LEADER: A title the publisher expects will have high sales. Large publishers give leaders significant promotional support, including money for advertising and author tours.

LEADING: The space between lines of type. Pronounced as "led," it is expressed as a *BASELINE*-to-baseline measure. Nine-point type leaded out at 12 *POINTS* will be written as 9/12 or phrased as "set 9 on 12." The space comes between the *DESCENDERS* of a line and the *ASCENDERS* of the next line. Type set 9/18 will have more space between lines than type set 9/12 or 9/14. Type leaded too tightly will be hard to read. The term derives from the narrow metal strips that separated lines of metal type in early typesetting.

LETTERPRESS: Today used most often for high-quality short-run jobs such as invitations and personal stationery, letterpress was the primary method of printing everything for 500 years, starting with Gutenberg. It was replaced for long-run and large jobs by *OFFSET LITHOGRAPHY* in the mid-1900s. Also defined as relief printing, letterpress uses raised printing surfaces such as those created by the Linotype and other *HOT-METAL* typesetters or by engravings.

LIBEL: Published words, pictures, or cartoons that are false and damage a person's reputation. Contrast with *SLANDER*, which is the oral communication of false statements.

LIBRARY BINDING: A reinforced binding offered by specialty binderies. Publishers ordering a large quantity of books bound for library sales may have them prebound; others can order extra covers to be used for rebinding paperbacks once their original **SPINES** are cut off. Names of some library binders can be found on the Library Binding Council website, *lbibinders.org*.

LIBRARY OF CONGRESS NUMBER: Identifies the catalog record created for a book by the Library of Congress. See *loc.gov/publish/pcn*.

LICENSING: Book text and images are often "sold" to other publishers (book, periodical, online) and to those who merchandise the book material (for example, as toys, games, and on apparel). More accurately described as an exclusive "rental," the sale is only of the narrowly defined **SUBSIDIARY RIGHT**, and only for a given time period. The publisher retains legal ownership of the material. In most cases, a licensing deal calls for publishers to be compensated on a **ROYALTY** basis. One variation of licensing is an option, such as for a movie or television series, which more often is paid for with a single fee. Most publisher/author contracts call for the author and/or illustrator to receive at least 50 percent of the royalty or fee. The Authors Guild, *authorsguild.org*, explains that publishers license rights for material they are not going to create: for example, paperback editions of children's books to be sold through book clubs. Many IBPA members have material licensed through such rights brokers as the Copyright Clearance Center, *copyright.com*, which handles transactions and collects payments.

LINE ART: Images created with a single color and without **HALFTONES**. Usually black-and-white drawings. Most **CLIP ART** is line art.

A lovely example of black-and-white LINE ART.

LINES PER INCH (LPI): This measures the resolution of a *HALFTONE* or line screen. The higher the lpi, the finer the screen and the sharper the image. See *DOTS PER INCH*.

The LOGO for IBPA

LOGO: A graphic representation of an organization's name. Often part of its graphic identity in *SPINE* artwork, letterhead, catalogs, and signage.

LOW-RESOLUTION: Low-res images can be transmitted electronically faster than higher-res images, but they have less clarity, especially when enlarged, and may look blurred. Images such as *STOCK PHOTO* previews are provided in low resolution for *LAYOUT* purposes; high-resolution images are necessary for book production.

LTL: Less than truckload, a freight term referring to shipments that do not require a full truck or trailer load. Less expensive than a parcel carrier such as UPS, an LTL carrier may provide residential delivery and/or lift-gate service.

MAKE-READY: The same as setup, make-ready includes all the tasks required to prepare a press (or other equipment) for a specific printing or binding job. In printing, this includes mounting *PLATES* on the press and adjusting the *REGISTRATION* and the quantity of ink reaching the printed piece. Each *SIGNATURE* of a book will require its own make-ready. One reason that jobs printed in black ink on *HOUSE STOCK* are less expensive is that make-ready takes less time and effort.

MARGINS: Unprinted space between the text or illustrations and the edge of the paper. The top margin is also called the *HEAD*. *GUTTER* is the term for the margins between two facing pages.

MARKUP: Usually expressed as a percentage, the difference between the price paid for something and the price at which it is sold. For example, a *WHOLESALER* that buys a book from a publisher for 50 percent of cover price may mark it up to 60 percent of cover price and sell it to retailers that mark it up to 100 percent of cover price, a margin (or in general business terms, a contribution) of 40 percent for the wholesaler. Retailers often talk in terms of discount (as in "from cover" or "from retail price") rather than markup.

MASK: A physical means, usually an acetate *OVERLAY*, of blocking a portion of an image such as the background so that the masked portion won't print. Masking can also be done

electronically, with programs such as Photoshop. Also called
KNOCKOUT.

MASS MARKET PAPERBACK: Paperbacks smaller in trim size
than **TRADE PAPERBACKS**, and usually somewhat smaller
than 5 inches by 8 inches. Sometimes distributed by firms that
handle magazines and similar racked products, they are often
sold in airports, drugstores, and supermarkets as well as in
bookstores at prices far lower than those of trade paperbacks.
Returns are usually credited when covers are stripped off and
sent back. Minus their covers, the books themselves are pulped.
Titles published only as mass market paperbacks may have
shorter lives than trade paperbacks. **ROYALTIES** for mass
market paperbacks are relatively low.

MASTHEAD: A copy block that provides a publication's name
along with information about ownership and staff and often
appears on the second page of a newspaper and on the contents
page of a magazine. Mastheads are valuable sources of editorial
contact information.

MATTE: A dull finish, the opposite of **GLOSSY**. Papers and
COATINGS can be matte or gloss.

MEASURE: The width of a line of type in a book, traditionally
expressed in **PICAS**.

MECHANICAL BINDING: Despite the name, "mechanical"
binding usually requires handwork, unlike **PERFECT BIND-
ING**. Examples include looseleaf binding, wire and plastic
SPIRAL bindings, and **COMB BINDING**, which is plastic.
Often used for notebooks, cookbooks, instruction manuals, or
other types of publications that need to lie flat when opened.

For sales in bookstores, most looseleaf publications are **SHRINKWRAPPED**. **WHOLESALERS** don't generally handle spiral- or **COMB-BOUND** publications unless they are boxed or have added **SPINES** that cover the spiral or comb so book titles will show when shelved spine-out. Plastic bindings are more easily damaged than other bindings and so are difficult to ship without special packaging.

MECHANICALS: Camera-ready assembly of type, graphics, and other elements complete with instructions to the printer, typically prior to electronic **PREPRESS**. A "hard" mechanical may also be called a **PASTEUP**, boards, or CRA (**CAMERA-READY ART**).

MEDIA: The plural of *medium*. Devices that package and transmit content, including printed publications, tapes and records, films and television, computerized data vehicles, and social media sites such as Facebook, Twitter, and LinkedIn.

MEDIA RELEASE: In publishing, usually an announcement of a new title, author appearance, acquisition, or personnel change written in journalistic style, so that media people can use it with little or no revision. Also called news release and press release.

METADATA: The Book Industry Study Group defines metadata as "structured information that describes, explains, locates, or otherwise makes it easier to retrieve, use, or manage an information resource." In the book industry, metadata is compiled by distributors and wholesalers, making dozens of points of information about a title available in their databases. They include title, author, ISBN, publisher, trim size, price, discounts, and more. See *bisg.org/product-metadata-best-practices*.

MIDDLE READER: A book intended for children ages 9–11.

MIDLIST: The term large publishers use for titles that they think will not be top sellers. Midlist titles are printed in smaller quantities than *LEADERS* and often have scanty marketing budgets. Books that would be midlist at huge houses can sell well through small and midsized publishing companies, where they get attention and time to develop momentum.

MOBI: See *EPUB* formats.

MOCKUP: A preproduction depiction of material. Often used for decisionmaking, mockups may show text from a manuscript in suggested typefaces and sizes or *GREEKED* text. A mockup accompanying a job to a typesetter or book manufacturer will show how the publisher expects the finished job to look and may include specific instructions; for example, with brochures, it may show the direction of folds.

MOIRÉ: An undesirable pattern in printed images resulting when *HALFTONES* and *SCREEN* tints are made with improperly aligned screens.

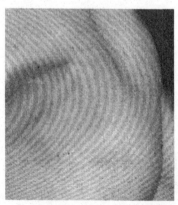

Improperly-aligned screens can cause a MOIRÉ pattern.

MONARCH: The 7-inch by 10-inch paper and accompanying envelope often used for personal stationery.

MONOGRAPH: A publication on one topic.

MONOGRAPH SERIES: A group of monographs, usually from the same publisher, each of which has the series title as well as an individual title. Monographs in a series generally have the same format and are often numbered.

MS: Manuscript, an author's work as submitted for publication.

NATIVE FILE: Book files in the desktop-publishing documents in which they were created. Many printers ask that publishers submit both native files (e.g., *QUARKXPRESS* or *INDE-SIGN*) and *PDF*s.

NEGATIVE LEADING: Type *LEADED* at fewer *POINTS* than the size of the type has negative leading. For example, 9 point type leaded at 7 points produces lines of type that are vertically squeezed. Extreme negative leading causes the *DESCEN-DERS* in one line to overlap the *ASCENDERS* in the next line.

This text is set 11/12 in Adobe Caslon with 0 kerning. Notice how it differs from text set with negative leading and negative letter spacing.

This text is set 11/10 in Adobe Caslon with 0 kerning. Notice how it differs from text set with positive leading and negative letter spacing.

This text is set 11/14 in Adobe Caslon with -8 kerning. Notice how it differs from text set with negative leading and positive letter spacing.

Examples of both NEGATIVE LEADING and NEGATIVE LETTERSPACING

NEGATIVE LETTERSPAC-ING: Reduction of the space between characters by *KERNING* or tracking, usually either to create a special effect (often in a title) or to squeeze all letters of a word into the same line.

NET INCOME: Income after ("net of") expenses. Because many publishers' contracts specify that *ROYALTIES* are a percentage of "publisher's net," authors may ask what these expenses can include. At a minimum, they will include book manufacturing costs, and usually far more. Depending on how a publisher allocates costs to books, expenses for a title can include editorial activities, text and cover design, marketing, and setup for or conversion to digital formats. Fees paid for illustrations, maps, and other **GRAPHICS** may also be charged against gross income. The way net income is defined can vary considerably from one publisher to another.

NONAPPROVAL PROOF: A proof sent by a printer for information only; the printer does not have to wait for approval before proceeding to printing. Nonapproval proofs are sometimes marked "For information only."

NONRETURNABLE: The industry term for a product that a customer cannot return for credit. **DIGITAL** editions and books sold to specialty retailers such as gift stores are often nonreturnable. See also **CONSIGNMENT**.

OBLIQUE: The slanted version of a type *FONT*, done to simulate *ITALIC*. Common with *SANS SERIF* fonts, which may not have italic faces. With desktop publishing software, fonts without oblique faces can be slanted manually.

OFFLINE BINDING: A binding applied after books come off the press rather than as part of the printing process; used for *PERFECT*, *SADDLE-STITCHED*, *CASEBOUND*, or *COIL-BOUND* volumes. Depending on the binding choice and the book manufacturer's equipment, binding may be outsourced. This is most common with *HARDCOVER* books and *LIBRARY BINDING*. See *BINDING*.

OFFSET LITHOGRAPHY: Usually referred to as offset or offset printing. A photographic printing technique that uses inks, carried by rubber rollers called *PRINTING BLANKETS*, to transfer images and type from metal *PLATES* to paper. To change what the press is printing, printers have to physically remove and replace plates. To change ink color, they have to clean rollers. Setup at each plate change involves making sure the correct amount of ink is being transferred to paper, and that the elements from each plate are correctly aligned (see *REGISTRATION*).

ON-DEMAND PRINTING: A process for printing one copy of a book or a relatively small number of copies as ordered. Now usually referred to as print-on-demand or *POD*. (On Demand Books is the name of the company that sells the *ESPRESSO*

BOOK MACHINE available in some independent book-stores.)

ONE-OFF PRINTING: Printing books on a **DIGITAL** press and assembling them in quantities as small as one.

OP, OOP: Out of print. The description of a title no longer available from its publisher because the inventory is exhausted and the publisher does not intend to reprint the title. Books may go out of print because the material in them is obsolete, the sales do not justify another printing, the publisher no longer has rights to the book, or the publisher has gone out of business.

OPACITY: A characteristic of printing paper that prevents "see-through"—that is, prevents what is printed on one side of a page from showing on the other side.

OPAQUE INK: An ink that conceals the color below it, whether it's the color of the paper or the color of some previously printed ink. By contrast, translucent inks combine with underlying color to create a third color. For example, if a cover is printed in yellow and then the title is **OVERPRINTED** in blue with an opaque ink, the title will appear blue. But if the title is overprinted in blue with translucent ink, it will appear green (unless a **KNOCKOUT** was used to prevent yellow from printing where the title will be).

OPTICAL CHARACTER RECOGNITION (OCR): The software that permits typewritten, typeset, and even some handwritten characters to be scanned and converted to **DIGITAL** code, enabling the creation of digital files of manuscripts and printed books. Commonly used for books produced prior to desktop publishing that are now being reset to be brought back into print. Scanned text usually requires significant editing, especially if the original material was set in more than one column.

OPTION: The right of first refusal of a manuscript or other piece of intellectual property for publication as a book or for use as the basis of a play, movie, or television production. Publishers' contracts as issued often grant the publisher an option on the author's next manuscript; authors may succeed in removing that provision during contract negotiations. When theatrical, movie, or television rights are optioned for a book, a fee is usually paid, and the period of the option is limited, perhaps with a renewal provision that carries an additional fee.

ORAL HISTORY: Primary source material in the form of recorded interviews or transcripts of them. Sometimes available from historical museums, academic libraries, and specialized archives. The Oral History Association maintains a list of oral history centers and collections at *oralhistory.org/resources/ centers-and-collections*.

ORGANIC: Website visits that result from something other than a paid search or a paid referral. For example, from a link in a Twitter post or on an author's website. Optimizing search engine results for a title, author, or company can reduce the need for paid search.

ORPHAN: Taboo in typesetting, an orphan is defined by the *Chicago Manual of Style* as the first line of a paragraph that appears by itself at the bottom of a page or column. It can also be a line of type less than column or page width that appears by itself at the bottom of a page. See also **WIDOW**.

OS: Out of stock, either permanently (OSI) or temporarily (OST). OSI is the equivalent of **OP**. OST means that the inventory of a title is depleted, but that copies are currently being printed, or there are at least tentative plans to make the title available again in print or **DIGITAL** format.

OTABIND: A brand of **LAYFLAT BINDING**.

OVER THE TRANSOM: Unsolicited manuscripts that authors send to agents or publishers they don't know are said to come in over the transom and land in the **SLUSH PILE**.

OVERLAY: Traditional **PASTEUPS** (aka **COMPREHEN-SIVES** or comps) are often sent with a tissue overlay on which corrections and instructions can be noted. When traditional comps have several elements that are to be printed separately on the same sheet, each element will be shown on a separate overlay, usually of acetate. Neither form of overlay is used with **DIGITAL** files.

OVERPRINT: Overprinting has several meanings. It is used to describe superimposing new information on previously printed sheets or blocking erroneous information in a previously printed job. It can mean creating a third color by printing one color over another, usually on a one-color press. And it can also mean printing more copies of a book than needed because a publisher will have other uses for the material. For example, a **SIGNATURE** of color photographs for a book might be over-printed to provide enough copies for both the first printing and an anticipated second printing. This reduces the unit cost of the color signature and thus the overall cost of each copy. See **OVERRUN**.

OVERRUN: When more copies are printed than were ordered. This may be done deliberately if the printer expects a high error rate for the job. Most printing contracts allow the printer to deliver (and be paid for) 10 percent less to 10 percent more than the quantity ordered.

OVERSTOCK: See *REMAINDERS*.

OZALID PROOF: A *BLUELINE* named for the company that created the technology for this kind of proof.

PAGE: A page is one side of a leaf, so a 32-page book will have only 16 leaves of paper. Abbreviated *p.*, as in *p. 2*, and in the plural *pp.*, as in *pp. 5–10*.

PAGE BREAK: The point in the text where one page ends and the next one begins.

PAGE COUNT: In book manufacturing, the number of pages in a book, including pages that do not have either roman or Arabic page numbers. In *METADATA* and for promotion, the actual number of pages that have content on them, including *FRONT MATTER* and *BACK MATTER*.

PAGE DEPTH: The distance from the top of the first line of type to the *BASELINE* of the last line.

PAGE PROOFS: Proofs that show pages as they will be laid out in the finished book. Sometimes the first set of page proofs doesn't include images; in this case, a second set of page proofs will be issued with all material included. With desktop publishing, *GALLEY* proofs are usually skipped so that page proofs are the first proofs created.

PAGINATION: Numbering of pages. With electronic prepress, pagination also refers to most of the page makeup work.

PAMPHLET: The traditional definition is an unbound booklet of 48 or fewer pages, but today the term can refer to a publication that has more pages, *SADDLE-STITCHING*, and possibly a cover of heavier paper than the text. The term does not refer to periodicals or books, although a short book might be formatted as a pamphlet.

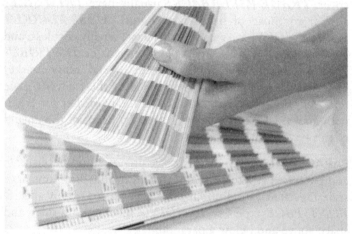

Fanbooks from the PANTONE® MATCHING SYSTEM

PANTONE MATCHING SYSTEM® (PMS®): This ink matching system is used to specify exact colors by color number and color formula. Most current *DIGITAL* color presses cannot match PMS® colors, but *INKJET* equipment being developed should enable PMS® matches. For a traditional offset print job, paper PMS® swatches can be attached to *COMPS* so that press operators can match printed output to the exact color specified. If an exact match is required, the publisher's bid request should specify this, as it may increase the cost of the job. Color monitors, laser and inkjet printers, and photocopiers cannot accurately represent PMS® colors.

PAPERBACK: A paperback book can be an original publication (paperback original) or a reprint of a **HARDCOVER** edition **PERFECT-BOUND** with glue and a heavy paper cover. **TRADE PAPERBACKS** usually have **TRIM SIZE**s similar to those of hardbound books. **MASS MARKET PAPERBACKS** have smaller trim sizes, usually cost less, and are often sold in racks managed by magazine **DISTRIBUTORS**. Instead of being returned, unsold mass market paperbacks are traditionally stripped of their covers; once removed, the covers are returned to the publisher for credit with an affidavit certifying that the text pages of the unsold copies have been destroyed.

PARAGRAPH STYLE: Word processing, desktop publishing, computerized typesetting, and web authoring programs have style tags that can eliminate the need to separately specify **FONT**, **FACE**, type size, **LEADING**, indentations, rules, and space above and below a paragraph.

PASS-ALONG READERSHIP: Periodicals' print media kits for advertisers and others cite "circulation" figures (the number of addresses receiving a copy of the periodical) and "readership" figures (also "total readership" and "pass-along readership"), which are always larger than circulation figures and based on estimates of the number of readers per copy. For example: "PW's print edition boasts 16,000+ subscribers with a pass-along rate of 4.2 readers per issue and is read by over 68,000 booksellers, publishers, public and academic librarians, wholesalers, distributors, agents, and writers" (*publishersweekly.com/ pw/corp/ advertisinginfo.html*). Unlike circulation, readership figures cannot be audited.

PASTEUP: *CAMERA-READY COPY*, created by pasting text and images printed on photographic paper on a carrier sheet. A pasteup (or *COMP*) can be photographed for the film negative that is used to make a printing *PLATE*. When a one-piece comp is required, the pasteup is photographed (traditionally with a *PHOTOSTAT* machine) for camera-ready art to send to a printer. With desktop publishing and electronic prepress, no paper pasteups exist.

PDF: See *PORTABLE DOCUMENT FORMAT*.

PERFECT BINDING: A binding method that glues a paper cover to book pages, and trims the entire assembly to create a square (or perfect-bound) *SPINE*. Most wholesalers and retailers do not stock paperbacks with other kinds of bindings unless the books are to be displayed in racks, such as those for children's books.

PERFORATING: A bindery process in which a line or border of tiny holes is punched in paper, often to facilitate tearing off a coupon. Perforating is also the term for cutting narrow slits in a sheet of paper to facilitate folding it into a *SIGNATURE* for *GATHERING* and *BINDING*.

PERIODICAL: A publication that appears more frequently than once a year, such as a magazine, journal, or newsletter. Many periodicals carry an *ISSN* (International Standard Serial Number), which is similar to an *ISBN* in that it identifies the publisher. ISSNs are not required for a publication to qualify for U.S. Postal Service periodical mailing rates. For more information: *usps.com*; ISSN International Centre, *issn.org*; and Library of Congress, *loc.gov*.

PERMISSION: Written clearance for publication of material from the owner of the relevant rights. Permissions and licensing for many publishers are handled through the Copyright Clearance Center (*copyright.com*), which lets publishers identify publications from which material can be copied, for what uses, and at what fees.

PHOTOSTAT: A photographic copy of a document, drawing, or *PASTEUP*. The name applies both to the copy and to the machine that makes it, which was commonly used before the advent of desktop publishing and electronic prepress.

PICA: Equivalent to 12 *POINTS* in the American print measuring system, or one-sixth of an inch (an inch being equal to 72 points). Until desktop publishing became common, picas and points were the measurements always used in printing.

A hardcover PICTURE BOOK

PICTURE BOOK: A generously illustrated book created for young children, usually with 24 or 32 pages and minimal text. Most picture books are large format (e.g., eight inches square or larger) and many are *HARDCOVER*. To reduce high printing costs, they are often manufactured in Asia.

PIRACY: The production or publishing of a book without permission from or compensation to the rights holder. The most common form of piracy in book publishing occurs when foreign printers either copy Western books for sale in their own shops, or *OVERRUN* jobs for Western publishers and then sell the extra copies, often at prices lower than those charged by the legitimate publisher.

PIXEL: Usually, the smallest single component of a *DIGITAL* image. The term can be used as a unit of measurement, especially when referring to *RESOLUTION*; for example, 2,400 pixels per inch, or 640 pixels per line. The more pixels used to reproduce an image, the more closely it can resemble the original.

PLAGIARISM: The crime of using someone else's concepts or words without permission and without acknowledgment. Publishers who suspect their material is being used by others can type phrases from their books into such search engines as Google Books as an initial step in uncovering plagiarism as well as piracy.

PLATES: Master surfaces from which printing is done, including rubber plates, *OFFSET LITHOGRAPHIC PLATES*, *GRAVURE* plates, and engraved plates. The term can also mean illustrations or photographs that are printed separately and inserted between text pages during binding.

PLATFORM: Usually means an author's platform—what the author has by way of a following, which might include a popular blog, friends and followers on Twitter, Facebook, and other social media sites, a track record as a speaker and/or a broadcast interview subject, and possibly a track record as a writer for large-circulation newspapers, magazines, and web publications.

Platform can also refer to a computer system, e.g., Macintosh or Windows.

PLOTTER PROOF: Like a *BLUELINE*, a low-resolution proof showing page layout and trim, and not representative of final color or quality.

POCKET: An envelope with no flap attached affixed inside a book, often on the inside back cover, to hold updates in textbooks, law titles, and the like, or to hold material such as patterns for a crafts book or a CD.

POD: See *PRINT-ON-DEMAND*.

POINT: The smallest unit of the American print measuring system used today, 1/72 of an inch. See *FONT* sizes.

PORTABLE DOCUMENT FORMAT (PDF): Introduced by Adobe Systems and originally made only with its Acrobat Distiller software, PDF allows documents to be transferred via email, *FTP*, or such physical devices as CDs. A PDF can be read on any computer that has Adobe's free Acrobat Reader software regardless of operating system or *PLATFORM*. Generic PDF creation software is now available, although it is not supported by all vendors. It is important to recognize that different print jobs may require different PDFs. High-end printing requires consultation with your service provider or book manufacturer for the appropriate specifications. According to Adobe (*adobe.com*), you may at a minimum be able to use the Adobe PDF preset called "Press" when exporting a document from desktop publishing.

POSTSCRIPT: Page-description language developed by Adobe Systems. In early electronic preproduction, book files were converted from *NATIVE* to PostScript files and then to *PDF*s.

POSTSCRIPT FONTS: A scalable *FONT* technology from Adobe Systems that renders fonts for both the printer and the screen. Originally, PostScript Type 1 was the standard for *SCALABLE FONTS* (those that allow all *POINT* sizes of a given font). Adobe kept a monopoly on PostScript fonts until Apple developed TrueType, later purchased and enhanced by Microsoft. Now PostScript and TrueType are standard for both Macintosh and Windows operating systems.

PP&B: Paper, printing, and binding is a printing industry term that describes the manufacturing costs of a book.

PPI: Pages per inch, a measure of the thickness of the paper stock a book is printed on and thus of the book's *SPINE*. Each paper stock may have a different PPI. The higher the number, the more pages per inch, and thus the thinner the spine. A book designer or manufacturer will use the PPI of specified paper stock to determine how wide spine artwork can be.

PREFACE: An author's introduction to a book, usually written in a direct, conversational tone and explaining what inspired the book and who contributed to the project. Another frequent element of *FRONT MATTER*, the *FOREWORD*, is written by someone other than the author, usually as commentary on the book's contents.

PREPRESS: The printing process after page layout and before completion of the printed piece. Today, most of this is done electronically. What the book manufacturer or printer may still handle is conversion of *NATIVE FILES* to *PDF*, if necessary, and *IMPOSITION* of pages into a *SIGNATURE*. For multicolor jobs printed offset, prepress can include the production of separations, negatives, and plates. Prepress can also include pulling proofs and adjusting the amount of ink flowing to the paper.

PREPUB: An abbreviation for prepublication, often used to describe marketing moves that should occur well before a book is officially published, or discounts available before a book's official publication date.

PREQUEL: Similar to a *BACKSTORY*, a prequel presents the story that occurred before the beginning of a novel. Prequels are often created after a novel has been successful enough to warrant a series.

PRESS CHECK: An evaluation of the quality of a print job, usually by the production manager or book designer at the time the cover and each *SIGNATURE* are printed. In a color print job, this requires that the production manager be present at the book manufacturer's site when each *PLATE* change is made. The production manager will check for such possible problems as *REGISTRATION*, *BLEEDTHROUGH*, and inadequate ink coverage.

PRINTABLE: As in "enable printable," a choice often appearing in *METADATA* for digital books. Saying "yes" means the publisher gives permission for readers to print pages from an electronic edition.

PRINTER'S ERROR (PE): A typesetting mistake. Unlike AAs (which stands for author's *ALTERATIONS* and is defined to include publisher's changes as well), PEs must be corrected by the typesetter at no charge.

PRINTING BLANKET: A piece of rubber that transfers an image to paper in the *OFFSET* printing process with the pressure of the rollers on the press. If rollers are damaged or not adjusted properly, they can cause the blanket to transfer too much or too little ink, resulting in such problems as inconsistency of color or coverage, streaks, and excessive *DOT GAIN*.

PRINTING PLATE: Used in *OFFSET* printing to transfer an image to paper, a printing plate may be metal, plastic, rubber, or paper. Typically, the plate is attached to a cylinder in the press.

PRINT-ON-DEMAND (POD): The process of printing books on receipt of an order (the demand), usually with a *DIGITAL* press and sometimes as *ONE-OFFS*.

PROCESS COLOR: Ink used in *CMYK* or *FOUR-COLOR* printing (cyan = blue; yellow = yellow; magenta = red; key = black).

PRODUCTION MANAGER: The staff member or consultant skilled in quality control of prepress and printing who evaluates the quality of proofs and does press checks, especially with color printing. See *EDITOR* and *PRESS CHECK*.

PROOF FOR APPROVAL: A proof sent by a vendor that requires approval from the publisher before the vendor can proceed to printing or *BINDING*.

PROOFREADING: Checking a manuscript or typeset material for typographical and other errors. Errors are noted with proofreaders' marks, including handwritten symbols and abbreviations. See the *Chicago Manual of Style* for a complete list.

Typical PROOFREADING marks

PROPORTIONAL TYPEFACES: Unlike characters created on typewriters, each of which takes up the same amount of space, characters created with typesetting programs take up different amounts. A lowercase *m*, for example, is likely to be at least three times the width of a lowercase *i*. With typesetting, a word with many narrow letters (*title*, for instance) will require far less space than it would have if typewritten.

PROPOSAL: The document created by an author to sell a book to a publisher, with or without the assistance of an agent; sometimes called a prospectus, a book proposal typically includes a table of contents, two or more sample chapters, a description of the market for the book, and information about the author's credentials and ***PLATFORM***.

PUBLIC DOMAIN: Text and images not protected by ***COPYRIGHT*** are classified as public domain. They may include material on which copyright has expired, material never copyrighted, or material not eligible for copyright. That material is in the public domain does not always eliminate the need for permission to use it or the need to pay for that right; if a copyright-free image is acquired from an archive, library, or stock photo company, for instance, permission to use that image must be obtained, and a fee may be charged.

PUBLICATION DATE, PUB DATE: Supposedly the date when a book is published and available for purchase. Although some online retailers do not show books as available prior to the pub date designated by publishers in *METADATA*, many books are actually in stores and being sold on the publisher's website and elsewhere months prior to pub date.

PULLQUOTE: Like a *CALLOUT*, a pullquote is a phrase or short sentence taken from the text and presented in large type in a magazine piece or book to attract attention to a given point.

An artistic and inspirational PULLQUOTE

A "quick response" bar code or QR CODE

QR CODE: The two-dimensional "quick response" bar code that consumers can capture with a smartphone or other wireless device, activating an application. Information stored in the bar code directs the application to a website that displays desired content and/or permits a wide variety of actions, including purchases. Although QR Code is a registered trademark of Denso Wave Inc., the Toyota subsidiary that invented it, Denso Wave makes it available for everyone's use, and anyone can create a QR Code for free. For online sources, type "qr code generator free" into a search engine. For more information, see "QR Codes: Reports from Early Adopters," via *Independent* articles at *ibpa-online.org*.

QUARKXPRESS: Quark Software Inc. design software for creating and publishing for print, the web, e-readers, tablets, and other digital media. A competitor of Creative Suite, the Adobe Systems Inc. software that includes InDesign.

QUERY LETTER: The query describes a book an author is proposing to an editor at a book publishing company, or an article an author is proposing to an editor of a periodical. Book query letters are designed to convince editors to ask for a full book proposal, usually including an outline and brief summary along with sample chapters. Authors should check each publisher's submission requirements before querying, and take steps to identify an appropriate editor to approach. Many publishers post submission requirements on their sites.

QUIET ZONE: Space before and after a bar code that must be white and blank so that scanners can correctly read the codes. A quarter-inch is typical.

Curly quote: " "

Curly apostrophe: ' '

Inch mark: "   Foot mark: '

Be sure to use the proper type of QUOTE MARK for the job.

QUOTE MARKS (STRAIGHT and CURLY): Quotations in typeset material are identified with "curly" quotation marks; the apostrophe functions as a single curly quote mark. A straight quote mark is used to indicate feet, and double straight quotes are used to indicate inches.

RATING: Used in broadcast commercial sales as an estimate of a program's audience size expressed as a percentage of the people in the market area. A rating indicates the potential audience for a single commercial on a specific program.

REACH: Used in broadcast commercial sales as an estimate of the unduplicated (unique) number of households or individuals reached during an advertising campaign, as in "reach at least 20 percent of the households three to five times during the campaign." Salespeople also cite "frequency"—that is, how many times the same people are reached during the campaign. Internet advertising salespeople also cite "reach" and "frequency" estimates.

READING FEE: The charge to review and evaluate a manuscript levied by some consultants, ***SUBSIDY PUBLISHERS***, and packagers, and by some agents who are not members of the Association of Authors Representatives, which prohibits its members from charging reading fees. A reading fee "can be a sign of a possible scam," writes longtime IBPA member Pete Masterson in his *Book Design and Production: A Guide for Authors and Publishers*, warning that the fees are a major source of income for some in the publishing industry.

READING (or READER'S) GUIDE: Titles intended for group use—in a classroom or a book club, for example—often include a section of study or discussion questions after the main content. Some of these sections provide additional information on events or eras mentioned in the book. Teacher's guides, which sometimes appear in the educator edition of a book intended for K–12 or higher-education students, may be required by public education departments at state or lower governmental levels that evaluate books for possible classroom use.

RECTO: Right-hand (odd-numbered) pages, from the Latin for right. (*VERSO* is the term for left-hand pages.)

REGISTER MARKS are crucial for proper alignment on press.

REGISTER MARKS: Symbols or crosses printed on original artwork to help with alignment during *PREPRESS* work and on the press.

OUT OF REGISTER

REGISTRATION is the exact alignment of two or more printed images.

REGISTRATION: Exact alignment of two or more printed images. Registration is important in jobs that involve printing in more than one ink color, and in all jobs with *EMBOSSING*, *DEBOSSING*, and *DIE CUTS*. When images don't align, the printing or die cut is "out of register." Publications created on large, fast web presses (newspapers, for example) may have images that appear slightly blurry because of poor registration.

REMAINDER: *OVERSTOCK*, or copies still on hand when a book goes out of print, are called remainders when sold at bargain prices to and through remainder dealers and booksellers. "To remainder" is to sell off overstock. Remainder dealers buy or broker the sale of remaindered titles.

REPRODUCTION: Prior to electronic *PREPRESS*, a photograph or *PHOTOSTAT* of *CAMERA-READY ART* could be used as a "repro," or reproduction proof. In publishing today, "reproduction" is more often used in the phrase "reproduction quality" to indicate the quality of text or artwork prepared for publication or already printed, as in "poor reproduction" (e.g., grainy, low resolution, colors not matched to samples or to specified *PMS* colors, or out of register).

RESERVES AGAINST RETURNS: Money due as *ROYALTIES* withheld by publishers to cover possible returns. Authors' contracts generally have a standard provision for reserves, which should be "reasonable."

RESOLUTION: A measurement of clarity. For a *DIGITAL* image, resolution is defined by *DPI*, which is the number of individual dots that can be placed within the span of one linear inch. If its resolution is not high enough, a printed image will be blurry. On a computer monitor, resolution may be as low as 72 dpi; on an *IMAGESETTER*, it may be in excess of 2,400. The ideal resolution for printing most books is 300 dpi. More often used in discussing reproduction of images, resolution can also be a challenge with small *REVERSED* type.

RETURNS: Most bookstores, book *WHOLESALERS*, and book *DISTRIBUTORS* can send books that are not selling back to the publisher. Returned copies that are shopworn or have damaged packaging are sometimes called "scuffs" or **HURTS** and usually cannot be resold as new, although putting new **DUST JACKETS** on **HARDCOVER** books can make them salable as new again. Damaged books are sometimes **REMAINDERED** or sold at reduced prices from the publisher's website. **MASS MARKET** titles and other books sold through newsstand distributors are often not returned; instead, their covers are removed ("stripped") and sent to the publisher, and all the rest is pulped.

REVERSE: Type or **LINE ART** that is the color of the paper it appears on because ink is applied to the background rather than to the type or image. With a job entailing multiple colors of ink, the background may be printed in a color or colors and the type reversed out (not printed) when another ink is added.

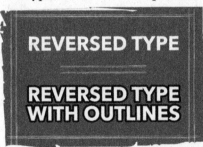

Type that is REVERSED out of a dark area, allowing the color of the unprinted paper to show through.

Reverses can be combined with **KNOCK-OUTS:** for example, if a book cover is to be red with yellow type, the red will be applied with the type knocked out (no ink applied to it) and then the yellow ink will be applied to the areas that remain the paper color. The knockout ensures that the second color will print accurately, and not be distorted by the background color. Reversed type is often outlined with black or a color. In small sizes, it can

Independent Book Publishers Association

be hard to read because ink usually spreads at least slightly, and if it spreads into the white areas of reversed type it is more noticeable. When color is applied to a reversed, or knocked-out, area, ***REGISTRATION*** must be precise.

REVIEW COPIES: Complimentary copies of books, sometimes called ***ARCS (ADVANCE READING COPIES)*** or ***BOUND GALLEYS***, usually in not-quite-final form and now often ***DIGITAL*** editions. Review copies go to media people and others who write book reviews, do articles featuring books and authors, and/or could otherwise provide publicity. To avoid giving free books to retailers or individuals who want copies for personal use or to sell, many publishers require that review-copy requests be submitted on company letterhead or with detailed background information. Some also stamp "Review Copy, Not for Sale" on the cover and ***BOOK BLOCK***. Copies sent to educators considering adoption of a book for a course are called ***EXAMINATION COPIES***. An instructor may be billed for the examination copy if the school or college bookstore does not order a given number of copies within a certain period.

REVISED EDITION: An updated and/or expanded edition of a previously published book, with changes made by the original author and/or illustrator or by a different author and/or illustrator. These changes may be within the text or in a supplement. A revised edition requires a new ***ISBN*** and other new ***METADATA***.

REVISION TRACKING: A feature of Microsoft's Word software, Track Changes allows an editor to indicate revisions made to a manuscript for the editor's future reference and also return the document to the author for comment.

RFID: Used in publishing primarily for inventory control, Radio Frequency Identification (RFID) systems consist of an interrogating transceiver and antenna working with an RFID tag (transponder) on a logistic unit or product such as a case or pallet of books. An RFID tag is a microchip with such data as title and quantity.

RGB: Red, green, and blue are the colors used to create images on monitors. All RGB images must be converted to *CMYK* for printing. This can be done with software such as Photoshop.

RIGHTS: The term pertains to licenses to publish material for the first time and licenses to use published material in whole or in part. For books, rights deals may convey first serial rights (for publishing excerpted material in a periodical before a book's *PUB DATE*), second serial rights (for publishing excerpted material after a book's pub date), and rights involving book clubs, reprints, translations, merchandising (for such things as toys, T-shirts, posters, and greeting cards), dramatization of various kinds, abridgement, audio, *DIGITAL* formats, and more. In book publishers' contracts, most of these are called *SUBSIDIARY RIGHTS*. Rights often revert from the publisher to the author when a book officially goes out of print, and reissuing older titles in digital format may require locating authors' heirs to obtain permission. Also see *OPTIONS*. And for a free downloadable checklist that you can use to define any and all rights deals, go to *bisg.org/docs/BISG%20Rights%20Controlled%20Vocabulary%201.0.pdf*.

RIGHTS CLEARINGHOUSE: A business or nonprofit that brokers *SUBSIDIARY RIGHTS* deals. One example is the Copyright Clearance Center (*copyright.com*), which explains that it handles rights for "in-and out-of-print books, journals, newspapers, magazines, movies, television shows, images, blogs, and ebooks." Publishers that license their content through rights clearinghouses can specify what content is available for what uses.

ROTARY PRESS: A printing press that uses curved **PLATES** attached to a cylinder, designed for fast, long-run printing. Most high-circulation newspapers and periodicals are printed on roll-fed rotary presses.

ROYALTY: Payment to an author, illustrator, or other **COPY-RIGHT** owner from a publisher. Royalties are sometimes a percentage of the cover price and sometimes a percentage of publishers' **NET**. No royalty is paid on **REVIEW COPIES** or **REMAINDERS**. Typically, royalty rates are lower for book club editions and other **SPECIAL SALES**. Royalties are not paid until any **ADVANCE** is earned out. Today author-services/self-publishing companies use the term *royalties* more loosely. Here's an example from one website: "Authors receive 40 percent royalty from direct sales ..." which may refer to the fact that authors get a 60 percent discount from cover price when they buy their books from this "publisher." Earlier this year, CreateSpace, an Amazon.com publishing unit, defined its royalty payments this way: "the list price set by the author/publisher minus CreateSpace's share equals royalty." That share could include 40 percent of the cover price for U.S. distribution through Amazon.com, plus a fixed fee based on the number of pages and ink colors, and possibly also a per-page charge.

RUN: Also "press run," a single printing session. Books printed only in black ink are usually printed in a single press run. Some presses require more than one press run to complete a multi-colored job, with each run adding a different color.

RUN IN: An editorial directive to make what was a new line or new paragraph a continuation of the line or paragraph that preceded it.

RUNNING HEAD: Also called *HEADER*. The line that appears across the top of a page as a brief identifier of content, often the book title on left-hand pages and the chapter title on right-hand pages. When this sort of line appears at the bottom of a page, it's known as a running footer.

SADDLE-STITCHED: Paperback publications with a limited number of pages can be stapled with either a wire or preformed staples, a *BINDING* method called saddle-stitching. Magazines and catalogs of 100 pages or less are often saddle-stitched. Because saddle-stitched publications have no spine, many retailers do not stock them unless display materials are provided (as they sometimes are with children's paperbacks, for example).

SAN: Bowker defines a Standard Address Number, which it sells, as "a unique seven-digit identifier used to signify a specific address of an organization in (or served by) the publishing industry. SANs are…required in all electronic data interchange communications using the Book Industry Systems Advisory Committee (BISAC) EDI formats." SANs are intended to reduce problems such as books shipped to the wrong points and errors in billing, payments, and returns.

SANS SERIF: *FONTS*, such as Helvetica and Arial, designed without (*sans*) finishing strokes (*SERIFS*) crossing or projecting from the main line or stroke in a letter.

Serif vs. SANS SERIF fonts.

SASE: Self-addressed, stamped envelope, usually required with an author's submission to a publisher so the publisher can return unwanted materials at the author's expense.

SCALABLE FONTS: Fonts that allow any point size to be specified with desktop publishing.

SCANNING: Creates *DIGITAL* images of illustrations, photographic prints, or text. Images can be saved in many formats, including *JPEG* for website use, *TIFF* for insertion in material to be printed, and *PDF* for *FACSIMILE EDITIONS*, often of out-of-print books for which no digital files exist.

SCORE: A line impressed into the pages of *PERFECT BOUND* books during the bindery process to make the pages easier to fold. Some pages are scored a fraction of an inch away from and parallel to the *SPINE* to allow covers to bend more easily.

SCREENING: The *PREPRESS* process that breaks a *CONTINUOUS TONE* image such as a photograph into *DOTS* for print reproduction.

SCREEN RESOLUTION: The higher the resolution of a computer screen as measured in pixels, the better the clarity of the text and images. A monitor cannot accurately show how clear an image will be when printed, especially if the image is a *JPEG* optimized for website display.

SECOND COVER: Books are sometimes produced with different covers, usually because a large quantity of the press run will be distributed by a single customer. When a book is being used as a giveaway, the second cover may include a phrase such as "This copy compliments of ..." If a bulk buyer has licensed book content for a certain market, the second cover might incorporate the buyer's name in the title: *The XYZ Company Guide to ...* A different front cover also creates the option for different text on the inside front cover, inside back, and back cover. (It's possible that second-covering a book might create the need for a different *ISBN*, to distinguish this version from the trade version.)

SECONDARY LEADING: Vertical space added above and below text elements such as quotations or bulleted lists.

SELF COVER: A cover printed on the same paper, usually a text stock, as the book or booklet within it.

SELF-PUBLISHING: The process an author follows to arrange, manage, and finance the editing, *COPYEDITING*, design, production, marketing, distribution, and sales of a book. Contrast with vanity or *SUBSIDY PUBLISHING*, which is author-financed, but not usually author-managed.

SEPARATIONS: See *COLOR SEPARATION*.

SERIAL RIGHTS: See *RIGHTS*.

Common SERIF fonts often used in typesetting books.

SERIF: The strokes used on serif type *FONTS* such as Bodoni, Garamond, and Caslon. Also see *SANS SERIF*.

SET-OFF: The same as "offset" when used to describe the transfer of ink from one printed sheet to the back of the next sheet going through the press, creating an unacceptable product. Causes include paper that does not absorb ink well, ink that is not absorbed well, and even humidity in the press area. ("Offset" in this context is not the same as **OFFSET LITHOGRAPHY**, or printing, although set-off, or offset, is more common with offset lithography.)

SHARE OF AUDIENCE: An advertising term referring to the estimated percentage of households or individuals watching or listening to a particular program compared to the number of broadcast sets in use when the program was aired. The higher the share of audience, the higher the cost of advertising for that program.

SHARE OF MARKET: Used to indicate market dominance, this is a percentage of a market that a given product or kind of product has—for example, the percentage of iPad sales compared to sales of all e-readers, or the sales of a certain publisher's **MASS MARKET** thrillers as a percentage of sales of all mass market thrillers.

SHEET-FED PRESS: A printing press that prints on sheets of paper rather than on rolls.

SHORT-RUN PRINTING: Printing a very limited quantity, typically 50 to 1,000 units for books. With **OFFSET** printing, short-run unit costs are very high; **DIGITAL** presses are commonly used for short runs.

SHOW-THROUGH: Printing on one side of a sheet that can be seen on the reverse side, a problem caused by lightweight paper or paper that is not opaque, or by ink wicking through paper.

SHRINKWRAP: Packaging made of plastic film, typically provided by a book manufacturer's bindery, that protects books through the shipping process and while they are on display. Book manufacturers quote prices for shrinkwrapping individual books or packages of books (say, the titles in a trilogy) or for "convenient," which usually means shrinkwrapping the tallest stack that the manufacturer's equipment can accommodate. "Convenient" is the least expensive option.

SIDEBAR: More typical in newspapers, magazines, and textbooks than in trade books, a sidebar is a short piece of text set off from the main text with information related to the main topic, such as a summary, an example, or a list.

SIGNATURE: A sheet of paper that prints multiple pages, signature also refers to the sheet when folded and trimmed into pages for one section of a book. How many pages there are in a

A 16-page SIGNATURE, which prints eight pages on each side of the sheet.

signature depends on the size of the parent sheet and the page size. Newspapers sometimes have four-page signatures (two leaves with a page on each side of each); book signatures are usually multiples of eight and often of 32.

SIMULTANEOUS (OR MULTIPLE) SUBMISSION: A manuscript sent to several potential buyers at the same time. The senders may be authors submitting books to agents or publishers, or publishers submitting books or excerpts to other publishers for subsidiary rights sales.

SINGLE TITLE ORDER PLAN (STOP): A discount plan created by the American Booksellers Association to reduce costs to retailers placing special orders for one or more copies of the same title with a publisher. STOP orders require use of the ABA STOP form.

SITE LICENSE: Now often a term that refers to electronic subscriptions or one-time purchases of publications that will be accessible to a number of users in the purchaser's organization. The publisher of reference guides might offer companies a site license for online access to a frequently updated publication, for example. Pricing may be similar to that of bulk purchases.

SLANDER: The oral communication of false statements that are harmful to a person's reputation, which may lead that person to take legal action. The written counterpart is *LIBEL*.

SLUSH PILE: Unsolicited (or *OVER THE TRANSOM*) manuscripts received by a publisher. To reduce slush, publishers can publicize their submission requirements on their websites and specify that *QUERY LETTERS* must precede manuscript submissions.

SMART QUOTE: See *QUOTE MARKS*.

SME, SUBJECT MATTER EDITOR: The title of the person who reviews a book's content for technical accuracy.

SMYTH SEWN: Refers to *SIGNATURES* sewn with thread before *BINDING*, usually binding as *CASEBOUND* books.

SNIPE: A very short promotional message, often shown across the top of a book cover or in the top right corner, and usually designed to appear as if it's been added to a finished piece.

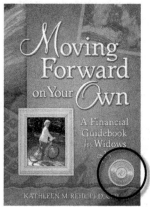

Examples include award medallions. A snipe printed only in black can be easily changed when the book cover is reprinted. Also see *VIOLATOR*.

SOCIAL MEDIA: Opt-in electronic media such as blogs and Goodreads, Facebook, Twitter, LinkedIn, and Pinterest that publishers and authors can use to post material about books and invite comments. Social media typically constitute an important part of an author's *PLATFORM*.

A printed award seal on a book's cover is also known as a SNIPE.

SOFTCOVER: Paperback.

SOFT PROOF: An electronically transmitted proof, usually a *PDF*. Electronic proofs cannot accurately display color as it will be printed.

SOLID TYPE: Type set with no extra *LEADING*, such as 12 on 12, or 12/12.

SPEC: Specification, as in "job specs." Specs that describe how a book is to be typeset and printed deal with *FONTS*, typefaces,

LEADING, ink colors, paper stock, and *BINDING*. As in "on spec": speculation; a term used to characterize a manuscript submitted to a publisher when the publisher has made no commitment to it. See *KILL FEE*.

SPECIAL CHARACTER: Any type character other than the letters, digits, and punctuation marks common in the language of a book. A publisher's and author's *STYLE SHEET* should include a special character list featuring, for example, accents and symbols.

SPECIAL SALES: A publisher's sales through nontraditional channels, such as nonbook wholesalers and retailers and organizations that buy in bulk to distribute copies to members, employees, or customers. Such sales sometimes involve *SECOND COVERS* for a title.

SPECIALTY RETAILERS: In publishing terms, any non-bookstore retailer; for example, a gift shop, baby boutique, museum store, or ethnic grocery.

SPECIALTY WHOLESALE: The wholesalers and *DISTRIBUTORS* that supply *SPECIALTY RETAILERS*.

SPINE: The back of a bound book. In a paperback, the thickness of the cover stock and the bulk of the *BOOK BLOCK* as determined by the *PPI* determine the width of the spine, and thus the maximum height of type and graphics that can appear on it.

SPIRAL WIRE BINDING: Corkscrew or spring coil wire inserted in holes punched in the binding edge of a book. Because of the potential for damage, booksellers seldom inventory wire-bound books that are not **SHRINKWRAPPED** or boxed. And because a wire-bound book lacks a spine, it will provide no information to readers when displayed spine-out in a bookstore.

SPLIT FOUNTAIN: In **OFFSET PRINTING**, a technique for simultaneously printing two colors from the same ink fountain. A full spectrum of color can be achieved at a one-color cost, but the press must be washed more often, possibly increasing costs.

SPOT COATING: Varnish or another finish applied to only part of a page, typically a front cover, to enhance a graphic element such as an image or title.

SPOT COLOR: A color other than black used for certain elements of a book's text, such as **SUBHEADS** or **LINE ART** introducing each chapter.

SPREAD: See **CHOKES AND SPREADS**.

STAMPING: Pressing a design, such as a simulated award sticker, into a book cover using **FOIL** or ink with a die.

STANDING ORDER: A purchase order for each successive issue of a publication, or each new edition or title from a publisher, until the publisher is notified otherwise.

STEAMPUNK: A subgenre of science fiction and speculative fiction that became popular in the 1980s. Goodreads.com says the term "denotes works set in an era or world where steam power is still widely used—usually the 19th century, and often Victorian era England—but with prominent elements of either science fiction or fantasy, such as fictional technological inventions."

STET: A *PROOFREADING* instruction directing that a change or a correction mark should be ignored and the text should be left as it was.

STOCK PHOTOS, STOCK ART: Images available free or for a fee from companies that license use of their own photos or images acquired from photographers and illustrators. Organizations other than stock art companies (for example, museums and libraries) also license images. Stock images can be purchased on an exclusive basis, so that other books or printed pieces cannot use the same image in a given medium and/or for a certain time period, which is important for publishers that don't want a photo on a book cover seen on other books, in magazines, or in advertisements. Fees for exclusive use are higher. Fees usually also depend on how a photo will be used, and in how many copies. For example, fees for a history book with a press run of 5,000 will likely be less than fees for an image to be used in a television commercial.

STOCK TRANSFER: The shipment of copies at a publisher's request by its *FULFILLMENT* agent to a destination such as the venue of an author event or to the publisher. Returning the publisher's property to it at the termination of a fulfillment agreement is not a stock transfer.

STROKE MENU: Desktop publishing programs such as *IN-DESIGN* allow type to be made bolder, or darker and heavier, by increasing the width of the stroke of each character. Outline type can be created by selecting a color for the stroke that contrasts with the body of the character. See *SANS SERIF* and *SERIF*.

STYLE: The spellings, punctuation, abbreviations, format for citations, and so on that are used consistently throughout a publication. Examples include the serial comma (or not) and the capitalization (or not) of job titles. A *Manual of Style*, published by the University of Chicago Press, provides the "house style" for many publishers. The stylebook published by the Associated Press is used by many newspapers and should be followed for press releases.

STYLES: In desktop publishing software, Styles are used to "tag" paragraphs or other elements of text with information that defines them. A novel might have one Style for chapter titles, one for paragraphs after breaks within chapters, and one for body text. A nonfiction book might also have Styles for **SUBHEADS**, quotations, footnotes, references, bibliography, index, and more. Styles should be used to define **FONT**, type size, color, indents, line spacing, rules, and paragraph spacing.

STYLE SHEET: The elements specific to a manuscript (see **STYLE**) compiled for reference during writing and **COPY-EDITING**, to ensure consistency and accuracy.

SUBHEAD: A secondary heading or title, often used to announce topics in the chapters of a nonfiction work.

SUBSIDIARY RIGHTS: See **RIGHTS**.

SUBSIDY PUBLISHER: A firm that gets a fee to print, and possibly also provide publishing services for, a title. Firms that promote themselves as "self-publishing companies" or "author services companies" offer subsidy publishing, often along with other book manufacturing and distribution services. Examples include Lulu, iUniverse, CreateSpace, and Lightning Source.

The publishing programs some booksellers offer in conjunction with their ***ESPRESSO BOOK MACHINE*** imprints are also subsidy publishing. Some subsidy publishers are better described as vanity presses.

SUBTITLE: An additional title for a book, usually explanatory. One of the sources used in creating this glossary was IBPA member Pete Masterson's *Book Design and Production*, subtitled *A Guide for Authors and Publishers*.

TEAR SHEETS: Now often replaced by online copies of printed or broadcast material, or by a *PDF* of a printed piece, tear sheets were originally print-on-paper copies of articles, published reviews, and the like. Requested by book publishers when providing review copies, tear sheets of reviews are useful as sources of comments about books to post on websites and to use in getting publicity.

TEMPLATE: Page *LAYOUT* information, usually saved in a desktop publishing program, that specifies text area, *MARGINS*, *RUNNING HEADS*, page numbers, and other design elements along with type and *PARAGRAPH STYLES*.

TEXT-TO-SPEECH (TTS): Creation of audible speech from computer-readable text. A TTS engine converts written text to a phonemic representation, and then converts the phonemic representation to waveforms that can be output as sound. The most important commercial applications are probably help desks and voice response systems that provide information such as account balances in response to spoken questions or questions via keypads. In publishing, the most common use is as an assistive technology—such as screen-readers—for the visually impaired and others who have difficulty reading. TTS is available for e-books, both through such hardware as e-readers and through software such as Firefox's Text-to-Voice (*addons.mozilla.org/en-us/firefox/addon/text-to-voice*).

THUMBNAILS: Small, rough sketches that show how a book cover, web page, or graphic image might look; valuable for exploring initial design concepts. Also, images of book covers or book pages shown in miniature.

TIE-IN: A new product created to capitalize on interest in an existing product, such as a book, movie, video game, or toy. A movie or television feature based on a book usually leads to a tie-in edition of the book, often with a cover using a photo from the movie or TV program and including photos from it. Dolls and stuffed toys of the characters in a book are tie-in products. Tie-in products are often cross-promoted with the work that they're based on.

TIFF: Tagged image file format, a standard graphic image usually generated by scanners. Capable of *HIGH RESOLUTION*, this is the standard format for graphics to be printed on paper.

TIP IN: Individual sheets can be tipped in—that is, glued into—a book after *BINDING*. Tip-ins provide a way to correct a problem such as incorrect text or images printed on one page, and a way to add material, such as high-quality color photographs, that must be printed on different paper and/or on a different press than the rest of a book.

TITLE METADATA: Descriptive information about a book, including *ISBN*, author, title, page count, *BINDING*, and text colors. *DIGITAL* printers and vendors usually want all title metadata submitted with the printing files. (For more about metadata, see "Desperately Seeking Good Data," Parts 1, 2, and 3, via *Independent* magazine at *ibpa-online.org*.)

TK: Abbreviation for "to come," an acknowledgment that some material is missing but will be provided in due time.

TRADE PAPERBACK: A *PERFECT BOUND PAPER-BACK* with a heavy paper cover, usually in a *TRIM SIZE* between 5 × 7 and 7 × 10 inches. Many trade titles are launched as trade paper originals. Titles launched as *HARD-COVER* books are often reissued in trade paper or as *MASS MARKET PAPERBACKS* that typically have a smaller trim size to accommodate the wire racks in which they are often displayed.

TRADE SALES CHANNELS: Routes to bookstores and libraries used by *WHOLESALERS* and *DISTRIBUTORS* that sell books they buy or consign from publishers. Contrast with *SPECIAL SALES*, *DIRECT MAIL*, and back-of-the-room channels.

TRANSPARENCY: Color positive film, such as a slide, which provides a better quality image when printed in a book than color negative film does.

TRAPPING: A prepress technique that eliminates white lines between adjacent colors in printing by *OVERPRINTING* each color very slightly.

TRIM, TRIM SIZE: The finished size of a book after *BIND-ING* and trimming. Many book manufacturers offer a limited number of trims. Especially with *PRINT-ON-DEMAND (POD)*, these may be only such standard sizes as 5 × 7, 6 × 9, and 8 × 10 inches. Unconventional trims and binding on the short edge can increase the cost of book manufacture.

TRUE POD (*PRINT-ON-DEMAND*): A book that is digitally printed after the order is received and *DROPSHIPPED* directly to the customer with or without the invoice included.

TYPEFACE: The characters that form a given type's "family," such as all the characters in Helvetica, Helvetica bold, Helvetica extra bold, Helvetica light, and Helvetica italic. Contrast with *FONT*, which is the type name, such as Helvetica, Times Roman, or Bodoni.

Helvetica
Helvetica Bold
Helvetica Extra Bold
Helvetica Light
Helvetica Italic

Several fonts within the Helvetica TYPEFACE.

TYPE GAUGE: A ruler, usually metal, calibrated in *PICAS* for measuring type. Also called a pica pole. Commonly used before electronic prepress measuring options were available.

TYPE SIZE: The size of characters in type is described in *POINTS*, although letters called the same size will not necessarily be the same size in different *FONTS*. This is especially true in terms of horizontal measure, because versions such as "thin" or "light" will be narrower, and versions such as "extra bold" will be wider. Some fonts also have shorter *ASCENDERS* and *DESCENDERS* than others. Today's technology allows for the selection of a wide variety of point sizes, and standard sizes can be stretched or *CONDENSED* with desktop publishing software's *CHARACTER STYLES*.

ULTRA-SHORT RUN: A *DIGITAL* print run and assembly of a very small number of books, usually 5–50 units.

UNDERRUN: The production of fewer copies than a printer's customer specified, either because of a press run that results in a lower quantity or because of a high rate of unacceptable copies.

-UP: A suffix indicating how many copies of the same cover or piece of artwork are printed on a parent sheet. *PAPERBACK* covers are often printed two-up. Standard-size postcards can be printed four-up on one letter-size sheet of *COVER STOCK*.

UPC, UNIVERSAL PRODUCT CODE: A standard product identifier that many nonbook retailers (such as drugstores and mass merchandisers) once required on books, since their systems didn't accommodate *ISBN*s. After ISBN-13s replaced ISBN-10s, ISBNs and UPCs became members of the same 13-digit identifier system (GTIN-13), making the use of more than one identifier unnecessary on books sold in nonbook channels. More than one identifier should never be used because dual identifiers and *BAR CODES* impede the ability to track sales. UPCs are available from GS1US (*gs1us.org*), founded in 1974 as the Uniform Product Code Council and later known as the Uniform Code Council.

UPPER CASE: Capital letters.

UV COATING: A shiny, protective layer sometimes applied to a cover after it has been printed. UV *COATING* enhances the appearance of uncoated stock and increases durability.

VARNISH: A thin, clear *COATING* applied after printing for protection, usually of a cover, or to enhance appearance or create a special effect. Varnish can be *MATTE* or *GLOSS*. A blanket varnish covers the entire printed area; a spot varnish highlights type or an image or simply adds a shine to certain parts of a sheet of paper.

VELOBIND: A brand of plastic *BINDING*, uncommon in *TRADE PAPERBACKS*; a low-cost alternative to *LAYFLAT BINDING* for cookbooks, teacher guides, and workbooks.

VERSO: Left-hand (even-numbered) pages, from the Latin for left. (*RECTO* is the term for right-hand pages.)

VIOLATOR: Signage that extends beyond (or violates) the edge of a package or a display, such as a starburst with a short promotional message that flares out from a cardboard *DUMP BIN*.

VOLUME: Printed sheets bound together as a book. Also, one book in a set or series.

WEB PRESS: A large press that prints on rolls of paper; used for high-volume jobs such as newspapers and magazines. Because web presses use paper rolls that are wider than the paper sheets *SHEET-FED PRESSES* ordinarily use, they produce either very large pages (as for a newspaper) or several pages for a *SIGNATURE* (a *TRADE PAPERBACK* printed on a web press might have as many as 64 pages per signature). Web presses use lower-quality paper such as newsprint. Since they run faster than sheet-fed presses, printing may be of lower quality, with some images not perfectly *REGISTERED*.

WET PROOF: A press proof printed with the *PLATES* prepared for a job and the paper to be used, to allow a final check before printing. Corrections and changes at this point are very expensive, requiring a new plate for every page changed.

WHOLESALER: Most booksellers and many libraries buy from wholesalers, which order books from *DISTRIBUTORS* or directly from publishers. Unlike distributors, wholesalers typically employ few salespeople. Wholesalers fulfill book orders that result from promotion done by publishers, authors, and/or distributors. Most book wholesalers buy on a returnable basis and require a *DISCOUNT* of 50 to 55 percent from cover price. Major wholesalers now also offer distribution services, at least for print books, and many distributors can handle book manufacturing and e-book conversions, either in-house or through contractors.

WIDOW: A short last line of a paragraph that appears at the top of a column or page. To be avoided. See *BAD BREAK* and *ORPHAN*.

WIRE-O: A brand name for wire *COMB BINDING*. Commonly used as an alternative to

Good typesetters will use their tools to avoid allowing WIDOWS at all costs.

LAYFLAT BINDING, usually for cookbooks, directories, journals, and workbooks; seldom used for *TRADE PAPERBACKS* unless they are *SHRINKWRAPPED* or boxed, and almost never for *HARDCOVERS* and rack-size *PAPERBACKS*.

WORK-AND-TUMBLE, WORK-AND-TURN: Used to describe what happens when artwork for both sides of a piece (such as a postcard or other advertising material) is arranged as a single image or *PLATE* to print on one side of a sheet, and then, after the sheet is turned over, to print on the other side. The sheet is then trimmed to create two or more copies of the finished piece. Work-and-tumble is easy today with the high-quality color printer-copiers used in many offices and in copy shops.

WORK FOR HIRE: Writing commissioned by an individual or organization that will own the *COPYRIGHT*. Someone writing on a work-for-hire basis may be compensated with a salary or with a flat fee rather than with *ROYALTIES*. An author employed on a work-for-hire basis may be listed as author or contributor or not identified at all. Work-for-hire is a legal category of the U.S. Copyright Act, and work-for-hire contracts must be carefully drafted. Payment of a flat fee does not in itself make anything a work for hire.

WYSIWYG: Pronounced "wizzy-wig," the acronym for What You See Is What You Get—computer displays that accurately represent what printed material will look like. Because colors are displayed as *RGB* and printed as *CMYK*, they cannot be WYSIWYG.

X-HEIGHT: The height of lower-case characters excluding their *ASCENDERS* and *DESCENDERS*. A larger x-height usually makes a *TYPEFACE* more readable.

x-height x-height x-height **x-height**

Each typeface has a slightly different X-HEIGHT.

YA, YOUNG ADULT: Books written for people age 12–18.

ZIP FILE: A file that compresses one or more files into a smaller archive so that the material will take up less hard-drive space and transfer more quickly.

ADDITIONAL TERMS

This space is reserved for you to add terms and definitions
you encounter on your publishing journey that
are not found in this book.

_____

_____

_____

_____

_____

_____

_____

_____

_____

_____

_____

_____

_____

_____

_____

_____